Desperately Seeking Me

'The Road To Bipolar Mania'

Mark Mansfield

chipmunkapublishing
the mental health publisher

Published by
Chipmunkapublishing
United Kingdom

http://www.chipmunkapublishing.com

Copyright © 2016 Mark Mansfield

ISBN   978-1-78382-252-2

Table of Contents

Introduction

Mark Mansfield is an amateur physicist with a diagnosis of bipolar disorder. That diagnosis came amidst an intense period of creativity, lack of sleep and increasingly bizarre behaviour, all of which were interpreted as an episode of mania. The effects on Mark's personal life were profound, leading to a criminal conviction, forced separation and divorce. During this time, he experienced a number of further manic episodes, including delusions and hallucinations. Thankfully the hallucinations have now stopped and with them the delusions too.

This book is an attempt to pick apart the various factors that led to mania. Mania is the signature part of bipolar disorder. Without it, a diagnosis of unipolar disorder (depression) is appropriate.

Mark Mansfield

The Facts and The Story

I'm aware that as a person with mental health problems, many of you will ask the question "is he for real". The prudent thing to do is therefore to open the batting with some facts and get onto the story later.

I invite you to check out the facts if you really think I'm a fake. However, I don't invite you to corroborate my story with any of the other parties involved. In particular, the main protagonist is my ex-wife and I seriously doubt she would wish to be reminded of any of the traumatic things that happened. So please take my story at face value and make up your own mind from there.

The Facts

My name is Mark Mansfield. I was born on 2nd July 1970 in Exeter in the UK.

I had a mild depression when I was 19 and left home. I was basically on my own and felt a great sense of abandonment even though I had made friends at my place of work and at home.
I married my first wife, Claire in 1995.

My eldest son, Thomas, died of meningococcal septicaemia in 1997. I was devastated and diagnosed with Unipolar Disorder (depression) in 1998.

I spent 3 months in the Bucknill Centre at Wonford House in Exeter, after trying to commit suicide with a kitchen knife. I received Cognitive Behavioural Therapy (CBT) and was put on a series of anti-depressants.

I came out of mental hospital and managed to recover, coming off anti-depressants in the process.

I had 3 more children during my first marriage, before getting divorced in 2010.

I met my second wife, Sue in 2010 and married her in 2012.

In late 2013 I was experiencing progressively more severe psychotic symptoms and generally manic behaviour.

In March 2014 I was diagnosed with Bipolar Disorder and spent 6 weeks on Delderfield Ward at The Cedars in Exeter.

Then in a string of manic / psychotic episodes, I was detained under Section 136 and then Section 2 of the Mental Health Act.

The police arrested me in October 2014 having slapped my wife during a manic episode.

I took an overdose in November and spent 3 days in intensive care followed by another spell at The Cedars.

I was given a criminal conviction in December and received a conditional discharge.

Sue divorced me in 2015.

The most severe psychotic episode happened in March 2015 where I was voluntarily admitted to mental hospital once more. I was having continual delusions and hallucinations. They changed my medication accordingly.

The most recent admission in June 2015 was also voluntary. This time it was purely stress-related and the manic / psychotic symptoms had stopped. They changed my medication once more.

Mental Health Disorders

Bipolar disorder is one of a number of mental health disorders. I won't go into details about all of them because I'm not qualified to do so. What I will say though is where I think there are some similarities with my condition.

Bipolar is primarily a mood disorder, with swings between manic (high) and depressed (low), hence why it was formerly known as manic-depressive disorder. During a manic phase, it is also possible to experience psychotic symptoms, which include both delusions and hallucinations. Delusions are where you believe something that is false. Hallucinations can involve any of the five senses, most commonly either hearing or vision. I can say that I have experienced all of these aspects of bipolar disorder.

Borderline personality disorder is not a mood disorder, but can involve very rapid personality changes, particularly when becoming angry and back again. In the simplest description there are at least two states, "angry" and "normal". In a more complex description there are five, including "protector", "punitive parent", "abused child', "angry child" and "healthy adult". Note that the personality states are not thought of as separate identities as such. There are a number of other traits of BPD and I can honestly say that I think I tick enough of them to qualify for a BPD diagnosis.

I had the discussion with my consultant and he still favoured the bipolar diagnosis because of the mood disorder element. This means I'm still on medication. Nevertheless he added "with emotional instability" to my medical record in recognition of what I had said about BPD and referred me to psychotherapy. He also said he hardly ever got anyone coming to him saying "I think I've got BPD" whereas he often got people saying "I think I'm bipolar", which is interesting.

Schizophrenia is another disorder which involves psychotic symptoms, so in that sense I tick the box. However, it is not a mood disorder so is probably not applicable in my case.

Dissociative identity disorder involves distinct identity states, driven by trauma in childhood. As I was not abused as a child, this would not seem to be appropriate. However, I keep an open mind that it is possible I have separate identities going on in my head. I've certainly experienced some traumatic things in both childhood and adult life and suffer from changes of personality. I also ticked a lot of boxes when I filled in a dissociative experiences questionnaire when I went for an EMDR (Eye Movement Desensitisation and Reprocessing) assessment.

As I don't experience flashbacks, a diagnosis of post-traumatic stress disorder (PTSD) seems unlikely. However, I am open to the idea of trying EMDR to see if it can help with some of the traumatic episodes I've been through.

The Story

The story that I'm going to tell is more subjective, based on my memory as well as my perception, both of which may be distorted. Nevertheless, I believe there is some value in my story because it conveys an idea of what was going on in my head in the run up to bipolar diagnosis and beyond. The manic behaviour, driven by psychotic symptoms including both delusions and hallucinations is the key element, without which a bipolar diagnosis would never have happened.

I hope that the story is of value to people both with and without bipolar disorder. In particular, if you're living with someone who seems to be displaying these symptoms, then this may encourage you to seek help from the medical profession. As someone with the disorder, one of the symptoms is that you tend not to think there is anything wrong with you and become very defensive if anyone suggests otherwise. Perhaps it is unlikely that bipolar people reading this will seek help as a result, but you never know.

Having recovered a little from some of the ravages of mania, I'm left wondering whether my bipolar disorder has actually been there all along. Reading about it on the internet suggests that the vulnerability has certainly been there all along. Bipolar disorder is only diagnosed at the occurrence of the first mania, so it's really a question of when that was. From memory and with the benefit of hindsight, I'd say that was actually during my childhood.

It is my belief that different states of psychosis are defined by beliefs in different things. In particular, it is when we start to believe something that most people wouldn't that manic behaviour progresses to psychosis. Likewise, when we start to experience hallucinations, many more beliefs can fit into the picture while we try to make sense of what we are seeing or hearing. This can reinforce the overall strength of a delusion and fuel mania some more.

As a person I am somebody who builds up an entire value system based on a structure of beliefs. Whenever I encounter a new situation, I re-evaluate my belief system to see if it's consistent. If not, then I modify it at an appropriate level and then carry on. If it's a low-level belief I'm modifying then the consequences can be dramatic.

From my point of view then I (usually) think I'm being reasonable, However, I've learned throughout my lifetime that what I consider reasonable and what somebody else does can be two different things. Or to put it another way, a person looking at it from the outside might say that the bipolar person has "poor judgement".

Given the series of things that have happened to me and that are documented in this book, I won't argue with the poor judgement label. However, what I will say is that even during psychosis I make judgements in a perfectly sane and logical way, given the information at my disposal. What I can't account for is whether the relative value of those things has become distorted because of a chemical imbalance in the brain. Hence the need for anti-psychotic medication, though I understand that many people are now questioning the legitimacy of the science behind all this.

Although psychosis doesn't appear to be happening any more for me, I will document my experiences from memory in an effort to shed some light on the role that beliefs have to play in all this. Then it's up to you.

Stressors and Delusions

From my experience, I'd say there are 2 main factors that led to mania:

1. Stressors. In particular, there had been a series of increasingly stressful events in my private life leading up to the time when mania was diagnosed. And with the benefit of hindsight I'd say that mania was evident at least 12 months prior to diagnosis.

2. Delusions. In particular there was one major hallucination at the bottom of my belief system that was supporting a number of associated delusions.

I take the view that mania is a symptom of delusions not the other way around. Whereas I believe delusions and hallucinations are symptoms of stress.

We can take a democratic vote on what's reasonable to believe and what counts as delusional, but at the end of the day it is a subjective thing. So I prefer to leave open the possibility that maybe some of the delusions were not delusional after all, merely unpopular. This makes my view of mania compatible with some other cultures, such as those that include shamanism, where delusions and hallucinations are treated as significant.

In the next sections I will describe the stressors, delusions and hallucinations that contributed to my mania. I also acknowledge that there is probably a life-long element to bipolar disorder which meant that I was already predisposed to it. In particular, I'd had a major depression 15 years earlier so I'd already bagged the unipolar diagnosis and was half way there.

My theory is that poor judgement only leads to a bad decision or a delusion if you go along with it. At every stage you have a choice. The act of making a bad decision or believing in something false (a delusion) is what invariably leads to further stress, which then fuels the mania some more.

For me this is what differentiates good from bad. If it leads to further stress then it's probably bad. However, bad may be only a relative thing if the rest of society deems the other option to be good. If you're in the business of developing a new theory about the world (which is what I do as an amateur physicist) then any new idea is likely to be seen as bad by everyone else. Such is the nature of the beast.

Trauma In Childhood

With all mental health disorders there is a natural tendency to ask whether the patient had a traumatic childhood. In particular, factors such as physical or sexual abuse can play a large role. I can happily say that I wasn't physically or sexually abused, so that would seem to make trauma less likely as an explanation. However, I believe that I did have a very traumatic first few months in life, based on stories that I have heard.

By my mother's account, my birth was a traumatic event. In the first instance I was late and didn't want to come out. And neither did my mother want to push, so they pulled me out by forceps delivery.

According to my Bowen therapist who I visited in 2013, the mild scoliosis I have to the left of my spine probably originated at birth. If they grabbed me by the shoulders and pulled me to the side so they could get the rest of me out, then this could have knocked my whole ribcage out of alignment. Apparently I had infant colic for the first 3 months where I was screaming my head off the whole time and she interpreted this as physical pain. I also have severe astigmatism, which could be related.

Furthermore I was given Cow & Gate milk to start with which my mother eventually deduced was too rich for me. She switched to Ostermilk and I slept for 24 hours solid.

Neither was I breast fed, so perhaps not much chance to bond with my mother.

Beyond that I can remember some other traumatic events in childhood, but probably nothing out of the ordinary and not enough to cause alarm.

My father was particularly strict and used to yell a lot and dish out spankings whenever particularly bad stuff had happened. I remember getting angry at how I was being treated, running outside and then jumping off a high wall to vent my frustration. Stuff like that.

Also he was someone that could only see things from his point of view, so I was "wrong" whenever I expressed mine. It was like walking on eggshells. And I got called names a lot. Perhaps this was enough of an "invalidating experience" to be a contributing factor for BPD.

On the flip side, both my parents worked and provided for me and my brother. This included paying for me to go to Exeter School, going on family holidays and the usual sorts of things.

I Was Being Reasonable

In general, my memory of my childhood is poor. I tend to remember specific episodes and then forget the rest. Apparently even this much is typical of psychiatric disorders, where the brain selectively remembers certain things and can store other things in a dissociative way so that they can't be remembered so easily. In some cases, full memory only occurs as part of a flashback, though I'm happy to say that I don't get those.

What I do remember is continually ending up in situations where other people, particularly my mother, thought my behaviour was unreasonable. Whereas I thought I was behaving perfectly OK. This is a theme that repeated itself in the run-up to bipolar diagnosis at the age of 44.

This particular episode is a fairly typical one from my teenage years, with possible relevance to mental health.

Although I can't remember all of the details of what happened that day, I can remember a great sense of injustice. Rather than feeling depressed about life in general, I'd spent the whole day arguing with my brother and winning for a change. I was feeling really good about myself, thinking that it was an unusual occurrence for me. And then my mother went and spoiled the whole thing by saying that I'd been absolutely awful and the sooner I stopped being like that the better.

In truth, I know I hadn't actually been physically unreasonable or anything like that. It was just a question of arguing and my brother had been arguing just as much as me. The difference was that I was standing my ground and not letting him get away with murder, which was the normal state of affairs and what was "required" to keep the peace. My mother had no concept of what was fair for me, only that she wanted peace because that was better for her.

So was I being reasonable? I would say I was in a manic state because I was feeling good about myself and this was an unusual thing. That clearly identifies a mood episode. I was arguing based on my beliefs. As I can't remember what we were arguing about, I have no way of measuring whether I was being reasonable or not. Suffice it to say that I thought I was being reasonable and my mother did not.

Confronting The Horror

Circling is a practice that offers a place where people can discuss issues or experiences that are close to their hearts. In this context, it can be a bit like group therapy, albeit with precise rules about how we express observations, feedback, feelings, understandings and so on.

One Thursday, I was privileged to sit in a Circle where some pretty intense personal feelings were expressed about a life-changing experience. This inspired me to write about the most significant of my own life experiences up to that point, which had been in the back of my mind for 15 years.

This draws on some memories that are particularly difficult to deal with, so apologies in advance if the ride is a bit bumpy...

The story starts at my previous place of work in Cambridge, where I turned up one morning around 9am as usual. The receptionist took a call from the hospital in Exeter, where my first wife Claire was in a very tearful state. She said that my son Thomas had been taken ill, was in a critical condition and that I should come straight away.

I promptly turned around, took a taxi to the station and got on the next train. The journey time was around the usual 4 hours but this time it seemed like an eternity. I remember being in tears as I had a sense that something was terribly wrong and the lady on the opposite seat tried to comfort me with some hopeful words and a tissue.

When I finally arrived at the hospital, I was warned that it wasn't looking good at all and Claire wasted no time in taking me to see Thomas. He was unconscious, covered in red blotchy marks, lying on a bed with various drips and bits of medical apparatus with doctors and nurses swarming around. He'd apparently lost consciousness a couple of hours ago, roughly about the time that I'd burst into tears on the train.

Somebody tried to explain to me what meningococcal septicaemia was all about and that this was a very serious condition, but it almost seemed irrelevant in the circumstances because I could see it with my own eyes.

The doctors battled to keep his vital signs stable for the next half an hour or so, after which a helicopter turned up to take him and his mother to St Mary's in London where the specialists were waiting.

So I then spent another 3 hours travelling back up to Paddington. I think someone drove me in a car but I can't really remember so I was probably already suffering from shock.

When I finally made it into the intensive care unit, I was told that they'd wanted to take a brain scan but had been unable to do so because of his critical condition. The nurses and doctors were all very nice and professional and conveyed a sense that this was somewhere that top quality care would be taken, which was a token bit of relief after the manic situation in Exeter.

The next 24-48 hours were spent with a very intensive round-the-clock care routine. Claire and I took turns to be there while the other one slept for a couple hours in the apartments opposite that were provided as part of the service.

During this time, I learned that the meningococcal bacteria acted like a million miniature chainsaw-wielding members of a drug cartel, circulating throughout the body and cutting holes in every blood vessel along the way. The blood leaks out of the holes before the body has a chance of repairing the damage, causing it to form pools in all sorts of places it wouldn't normally be, including under the skin. This causes characteristic red blotches a bit like a tattoo that don't go away when you press a glass against the surface of the skin (unlike acne, chicken pox or any other inflamed spot-forming disease where the redness is part of normal blood flow).

Thomas had a lot of red blood marks in his hands and feet, particularly the fingers and toes. I was told this was an example of a fairly bad case of septicaemia. The milder form of viral meningitis causes seriously bad headaches and can also be fatal, although many of us carry the virus around in our bodies without it ever developing into anything harmful.

After the first couple of days, there was a sense of hope from the fact that his vital signs were improving. He was still unconscious, but his body (with the help of ordinary penicillin) had healed up the damage to the blood vessels, his blood pressure was better and he was no longer considered to be in immediate danger. I remember the nurses and doctors becoming more relaxed and Claire and I took comfort from their optimism.

However, we did have to face the rather more gruesome reality that many of his fingers and toes were starting to shrivel up as his body was learning to divert the blood flow elsewhere. We were told that yes, they would drop off, that in particularly bad cases people might lose hands, feet or even whole arms and legs and yet still survive.

A few days later we were confronted with the full horror of Thomas's situation. His pupils started to dilate and the doctors and nurses rapidly went from being quite relaxed to a state of maximum alarm. They then decided to do the brain scan that they'd been unable to do at the start of the week and the results were devastating. He'd suffered massive brain damage, probably in the first few hours of the illness and had no chance of survival. Although they'd spent over £100,000 keeping his body alive for a whole week, his brain was now dying and the best thing to do was to remove the oxygen and drips that were keeping him going.

He died in his mother's arms a few minutes later, at the age of 16 months.

Rest in peace, Thomas.

I never had the chance to comfort you while you were still conscious and I will always love you.

My Leg Was Going To Drop Off

After I'd experienced a severe depression following the loss of Thomas, I'd taken up running at lunchtime as a way of managing my mood without anti-depressants.

I enjoyed it for many years, with the distances growing gradually over time. Then the inevitable happened and my running partner, Martin, decided he wanted to train for a marathon. I agreed to do likewise and we got on with it. I got as far as 23 miles before I tore my left hamstring. Needless to say that put paid to any chance of running on the day.

I really struggled with the recovery and was in a lot of pain. It was seemingly taking over other parts of my body too. In my mind, the injury was spreading to these other places and that's what was causing the pain. I had no idea that the pain mechanism itself was to blame for returning faulty information. Armed with my beliefs, it seemed like my leg was suffering an injury way more severe than a simple hamstring tear. Eventually, when the pain spread to my chest, I was convinced that I would not be able to breathe any more.

At this point I called an ambulance. They measured my heart because I was in such an agitated state, but luckily for me I have a strong heart so there was nothing to worry about,

Eventually I ended up in hospital, unable to walk. The doctor thought a little about the situation, got me to stand up with his assistance and then to take a few steps. He said that I would experience a lot of pain during recovery, that it was OK to walk on it and only by walking on it would I heal up. That was all I needed to know. I replaced the belief, that what my body was telling me was true, with the belief the Doctor had given me and I was on my way to a full recovery.

The Viking Within Me

This is going to sound a bit off-topic, but if you'll spare me a few moments, there is a point behind it all. I recently acquired a fantastic item from the great online car-boot sale that is eBay. It's an authentic late 17th century document relating to the city of Exeter and has a description that I find absolutely fascinating...

It starts with "Exeter is a city of great antiquity and fame, renowned for its loyalty and zeal for monarchy amidst all revolution." Clearly whether you were on the side of the King or not was a really important issue back then, and my second wife Sue's son joked that she was doing a good job of upholding the zeal for monarchy today. It then goes on about "King Athelstan" and gives a description of the main landmarks, which are basically the cathedral and Rougemont castle, which had been repurposed to house the courts. So it was very much the same then as it is now.

Later on though the tone gets a lot darker and it tells us about the "Danes" (i.e. the Vikings). Apparently Exeter suffered a great deal with Viking raids and was sieged many times. Although the citizens always put up a great fight, the invaders invariably won and then went on to rape and pillage throughout the city.

Reading this latter part sent a real chill down my spine. Learning about the Vikings at school had been kind of fun and interesting and somehow the "rape and pillage" part had happened to somebody else and was a million miles from me. But now I've learned that this atrocity went on many times in the very city that I've lived for most of my life, albeit a thousand years or so earlier. It occurred to me that maybe one of my ancestors was raped by the Vikings and so it's possible there's some of that blood surviving in me today. For those of us that believe in karma, that's quite a scary thought!

Interestingly, Sue had received a psychic reading a year or so previously which spoke of some bad karma, dating from Roman times, that would be rearing its ugly head as soon as we got married. Sure enough, the next year of our lives was absolute hell thanks to multiple members of my family behaving like complete assholes towards both Sue and myself. So the psychic lady clearly predicted that bit accurately. However, having re-read the Exeter document, I'm half wondering whether she got her history wires a bit crossed and actually it was Viking bad karma rather than Roman.

In truth, I have no idea whether my family tree really goes back that far within the bounds of the city of Exeter. When my mother meticulously traced it back several generations she found it very difficult to follow it back any earlier than the document I have in my hands. Perhaps I could get a DNA test done that would tell me the answer one way or the other... but I digress.

The really interesting part for me comes up when I consider my own character. If I'm completely honest about it, I notice that there are 2 very distinct sides to it. One side is quite placid, easy-going and non-confrontational. I can imagine this being consistent with the native inhabitants of the city of Exeter, with a history of farming, the woollen trade and so on. This is my everyday persona which does me quite happily for 99% of the time.

However, the other side can be quite spiky and argumentative and if pushed can respond in a very nasty and confrontational way. I know that we're all capable of behaving a bit like this, but I'm also aware that my version of it can be particularly pointed, despite my best efforts at personal development via counselling, cognitive therapy, Bowen therapy and now Circling.

I admit that I have found it very difficult over the years to reconcile the 2 wildly different parts of my character, having suffered with depression several times and taking a somewhat bizarre route through some life experiences to get to this point.

The good news is that I genuinely believe I'm making some progress. Circling has really accelerated the process in the last 6 months and my friend Ben has been instrumental in pointing out various sharp bits as part of his feedback to me, drawing from his training with Decker et al in San Francisco. Even the Authentic Games session brought out yet another aspect of my pointy behaviour that I can now work on.

So I would like to offer a warm heart-felt thank-you to Ben and to all of the guys and girls who have been involved in Circling UK and the Authentic World movement to date. Yours is the most effective personal development technique I know of and if it can reconcile the Vikings with the farmers then it is powerful indeed.

Going To War With My Parents And First Wife

During my first marriage, relationships with my parents had been a little strained. They'd been divorced since I was 19 years old and both remarried, although neither of them invited me to their respective weddings. And they had a habit of maintaining relationships with Claire and not with me, which I found irritating. For his part, my father accuses me of not inviting him to any of the children's parties. However, Claire insists that she did invite him to several, but got fed up when he never turned up because he was building a house at the time. It took 20 years to complete and even then had stuff that still needed doing.

When I got divorced, I expected that things would shift around in my favour, but was horrified to find that my parents were more interested in maintaining a relationship with my first wife than with my second wife. Sue was horrified too, needless to say.

Sue had a run-in with my mother as soon as we bought a house together. All of a sudden my mother was interested in coming round so she could see the children, but she made sure that she was in control of what was going on and Sue didn't get a look in. It was at that time that Sue made a mistake by saying something along the lines of me having doubts about the relationship with my father. She thought she was speaking in confidence and never in a million years expected my mother to go and report this directly to my father.

At this point, Sue's parents had been introduced to my mother but not to my father. We went on a large holiday in St Lucia with all 5 of our children, where we tied the knot. We'd intended to introduce to my father when we got back.

When we did get back, it was as if the world caved in. We'd had an absolutely lovely time in St Lucia, but it came to a rapid halt as soon as we got back to the UK. My mother started it off by being particularly offish towards Sue and her parents. And then I tried to phone my father. After a series of rebuffs and various excuses, it was clear to me that he just wasn't interested. Sue's parents were horrified and rightly so. So was I.

The other issue was that prior to getting married Sue and I had made it clear to my father and his wife Sara that Sue would be keeping her name Mansfield, largely for business reasons. Yet they sent a cheque payable to both of us in my surname. This appeared to be a deliberate snub to Sue and I was so annoyed that I subsequently changed my name to Mansfield.

So the next day I went to war with my father, not knowing that because of the direct line between him and my mother and brother, I would soon be going to war with all of them.

I had a blazing row with him on the phone. Admittedly, I completely lost it and said a series of things that would have been highly offensive to him. He was good enough to agree to meet me later on while we discussed it all more rationally. That was the last time I was invited to his house. It was not as if the discussion went particularly badly as there were some positive things in there and only a couple of things where I was holding my line, regarding how he had behaved towards me in childhood. We're talking verbal abuse here and some excessive spankings. Interestingly, I subsequently read a book which said that with abusive / co-dependent parents, if the abuser is challenged later in life, they will explode in a fit of rage and then go through a depression without apologising. This is exactly what happened over the next few months.

I phoned my mother to warn her that she may hear about things from my father. She informed that she already knew and that I should be absolutely ashamed of myself for accusing my father in this way. Blimey. I thought they were divorced, but it was like going up against the Mafia all over again.

As luck would have it we all met up a few days later in Teignmouth for a dance show with my eldest daughter. The atmosphere in the lobby was as if someone had died. My father and his wife Sara were all but ignoring us. My mother was in outright militant mode, having organised 2 rows of seats where she insisted everyone would be sitting. And her husband, Pete, took Sue aside and told her that I was a head case and should be on my medication. Never mind the fact that the only thing I'd been diagnosed with up to this point was depression. Sue basically told Pete where to go.

Initially Sue and I went along with it. Then judging from the mood, decided we were not comfortable so got up and sat down nearer the front. I later heard a comment from my father that we had behaved "like children". Yet he and Sara were the ones that had blanked us on the way in.

When we got to the interval, we went out to the lobby again. My mother appeared in a more hostile mood than I had ever seen her.

She absolutely blasted for not sitting down and talking to my father. I was so incensed that I blasted her back for the way I was being treated and that whatever I'd said to my father was between me and him, none of her business. Interestingly, the next time I saw my mother, she outright denied that this conversation in the lobby had ever taken place. So we're either talking about someone who is economical with the truth, or really does have selective memory.

This wasn't the end of it though because apparently my mother then headed off to the ladies, where she encountered Sue at the hand dryer. She remonstrated with Sue, presumably along similar lines to the conversation she'd had with me. And then she grabbed Sue by the arm. At this point Sue decided that enough was enough and told her where to go.

The next person to enter the fray was my brother, Paul. Sue and I had invited him to our wedding party at our house. We deliberately didn't invite my mother or my father for obvious reasons. So guess what, Paul made sure he had a full briefing from both parents before he came round. The first half of the evening went well enough, when the children were in attendance. As soon as they'd left, I had a conversation with my brother and he opened up with both barrels, telling me how both Sue and I were bad people. The other guests were shocked. In particular, the policeman and the marine who were in attendance made sure that when I escorted Paul outside, they went with me to see that a fight didn't break out. My brother left, but by this time the damage had been done and Sue was in tears. She couldn't believe what a horrid family she'd married into. The following day Sue even took a phone call from Paul where he accused her of being "Psycho Sue". The irony was clearly lost on him that he was the one being abusive.

The next time we saw my mother was at her house. Sue and I had gone round in an attempt to talk directly about what happened to see if some common ground could be found. My mother just denied, denied, denied. Peter was getting very hostile saying that we were upsetting an old lady. Having seen my mother lie directly about the incident in the lobby, I didn't doubt that she was also lying about the incident in the ladies too, as Sue was claiming. Pete said that I should leave and take my bitch of a wife with me.

After this we decided to have some counselling with Brian at Relate. He advised to ignore the situation with the parents and focus on our relationship and the children.

The final person to enter the fray was Claire. As I'd been having a difficult time with my eldest daughter since the time of her birthday in December, she'd been staying with Claire and refusing to see me. I was getting more and more exasperated by her behaviour. In the end, I asked what seemed like the obvious question ... was she really my daughter?

Claire reacted by taking all three children away from me and issuing me with a solicitor's letter. My stress levels reached an all-time high, which was the precursor to my Derren Brown delusion.

Over the next few months, I argued the case to and fro. To the disgrace of both me and her, the argument didn't end until a DNA test organised by the CSA settled the matter once and for all. Basically Claire had decided to go to the CSA for maintenance payments despite the fact that I had a 100% track record. The result was that my daughter is my daughter with nearly 100% certainty.

The next time I saw my father was in a pub in Thorverton. I wasn't allowed to come round to the house or even make a phone call, I had to send him an email. The things we'd discussed the last time we'd been in his house were all forgotten. He was on the war path against me and was absolutely fuming that I'd implied he was a liar regarding the arrangements to see Sue's parents. He was shaking, going red in the face and banging his fist on the table. I remembered the prediction from the book. Honestly, it was like watching an episode of CSI where they try to get the suspect to confess. I got up to leave. He looked up at me and I think he understood the implication - that if I walked out the door he wouldn't be seeing me again. So he changed his tune, I sat down and we talked some more. We left it so that it was at least possible to talk some more, albeit in neutral territory. Apparently Sara hated my guts for what I'd done to him, which left me in no doubt as to who was really pulling the strings here. I've never seen her since the incident in Teignmouth.

The war with my parents has had some benefits though. Once my relationships with my younger two children had been re-established, they seemed better than ever. Whereas before they would argue all the time and get bullied by my eldest daughter, now they didn't seem to argue at all. And when I did finally rebuild the relationship with my mother about a year later, it seemed to be on better terms. Relations with my father continue to be strained and at the level of email only if initiated by me. And my brother is staying in Wales so I hardly ever see him.

Mark Mansfield

Estranged From My Eldest Daughter

The troubles had really started when we lived in a cottage in Countess Wear, prior to moving into the house in St Thomas. My eldest daughter was behaving aggressively towards Sue and Sue barged her down the sofa in return. Then my daughter slammed the gate on Sue while we were out cycling.

When we went camping, a massive argument flared up regarding a missing swimsuit with my daughter accusing both Sue and I of causing her to lose it. I took her back to her grandmother's for a few days to let her cool off. With the benefit of hindsight, this was probably excessive, but I was aware just how much tension there was between her and Sue.

Some months later she became a bit more withdrawn and I was worried about her. I phoned Claire for support and basically got told where to go. That there was nothing wrong with my daughter and I was the one with issues.

In the run-up to her birthday in December 2012 my daughter had been behaving a bit like an uber-teenager, at least when she was around me and Sue. When we went to the church for the carol service in Kenton, she basically blanked us, despite wearing a coat that had been bought for her by Sue. I was incensed.

On the day of her birthday I wished her happy birthday and she ignored me. Actually she ignored everyone in the house. Apparently I hadn't said happy birthday when I passed her on the way down to breakfast and that was the end of the world. We went shopping and she was a bit better, then we came back for lunch.

I asked her to help with the washing up along with everyone else. She refused and went upstairs. At that point I lost it and called upstairs for her to come outside with me.

I remonstrated with her, saying that she had to try harder with other people rather than ignoring them. I said she was doing fine with her school work but was doing really badly in social situations. And then I did something which I regret to this day. I called her a "lazy toe rag". This was the first and only time I ever called her a name. Given how much I objected to my father calling me names, I am ashamed that I made the same mistake as part of my "punitive parent" behaviour.

Then I said I was sending her to her mother's for a month and was cancelling the birthday meal with a friend that we had organised for later. Little did I know she would never be coming back.

Sue and I spent Christmas in Portugal with her parents. I tried phoning Claire but my daughter refused to speak to me on the phone.

Over the next few months, I tried all manner of ways to get in contact with her, but she just refused or burst into tears apparently. It wasn't helped by Claire's passive-aggressive behaviour where she would just ignore my phone calls and text messages, so I fell out with her on more than one occasion.

After several months and having attended a number of Circling sessions, I wrote a piece which expressed how I was feeling. I never sent this to my daughter so I am reprinting it here instead.

Hi Sweetheart,
I am writing to you because I realise there are powerful forces that surround us. They have their origin in our identities as individuals, tangle together to form our personalities and interact via the relationship between us.

We have been drawn into conflict, partly as a result of our own forces, which are within our control and partly because of external influences which are not. I am missing you terribly and feeling great pain because of our separation. I imagine that you are feeling the same and so I'm doing my utmost to resolve the conflict sooner rather than later.

I am a warrior of the truth and the written word is my sword. It is a sharp implement and can have both fantastic and terrifying consequences, so I seek to use it wisely.

My identity has its roots in my ancestral DNA, my upbringing as a child and my journey through adult life. I am growing as an individual and so are you.

When our personalities come into conflict, sparks can fly. As an adult I accept that the collision may send us in opposite directions.
I just wanted you to know that I love you to bits and I'm praying that you will come back to me.
Dad x x x

Derren Brown Was Interfering With My Life

I had seen and enjoyed Derren Brown on TV. And my wife Sue wanted to see him in Torquay. So he was in my thoughts when I observed a number of strange things.

The first incident was on a bank holiday where trying to find a garden centre that was open was proving to be a major challenge. We'd driven from Exeter to Bow, only to find that it was closed. So we turned around and drove back to Cowley, only to find that one was closed too. I'd just about turned around and was about to drive out onto the main road once more, when 2 cars approached simultaneously, one from each side. Each one turned into the space between the main road and the gate where I was waiting, drove around me and then headed back off in the direction from which they'd come. It was as though someone had sent 2 cars to intercept me at the exact same time and the only person I could imagine wanting to do that was Derren Brown, as part of one of his experiments.

Although there was no particular upshot from the simultaneous cars, the thought of Derren Brown stuck in my head and resurfaced at the next opportunity.

In this case, it was quite a complex situation. I'd fallen out with my eldest daughter and sent her back to her mother. Then after she showed no sign of improvement, I'd questioned whether she was my daughter at all, at which point Claire used a solicitor to take all 3 children away from me. In a state of stress, I'd driven to the police station and accused her of murdering our first child. After the police escorted me back home, I was in the lounge discussing things with Sue's father. I referred to the fake meteorite that I'd bought him off eBay and he then questioned what I believed was going on. This was enough to trigger the Derren Brown belief all over again, only this time with him controlling everything.

I remember experiencing a weird shift as I entered a kind of alternative reality where we were all participating in a TV show organised by Derren Brown. Initially I was reluctant to go with it, then I sort of rolled my eyes to the ceiling with the resignation that I was going to see how this played out.

I sat on the sofa and started talking to Sue's father. I can't remember what we talked about or for how long, but I remember scanning the room for TV cameras and trying to figure out what everyone's role was. Sue was repeatedly coming up and down the stairs, explaining that someone was on their way.

Eventually the mental health crisis team arrived. We talked about things, I gave the doctor as much information as I had, including a discussion of my imagined reality TV show. I was also checked over by one of the doctors and the general conclusion was that I was experiencing a psychotic episode. I was waiting to "win" the show and for someone to introduce me to Derren Brown next, but this did not happen.

Eventually everyone left the lounge apart from Sue's father. I got up to go to the loo, asked him whether there were any TV cameras there and he assured me there were not. At this point the weird shift happened again and I returned to normality.

Stormy Times With My Second Wife

It's no surprise that with all of the shenanigans going on with everyone around me that Sue ended up absorbing some of the stress herself. In fact her direct interactions with these people were no better than mine. That put together with the usual stresses and strains in any relationship meant that our marriage was a recipe for arguments.

Looking back, the arguments started quite early on in our relationship, soon after we first met. We were going to salsa classes in Torquay and that was the source of some anxiety for Sue because I was dancing with other women. She would get concerned that I was wanting more than just dancing from them and would express those concerns when we got home. Also on a number of occasions we were scheduled to go to salsa but she decided on the night that she wasn't feeling well enough, which was disappointing to me. If I dared to suggest that I went on my own, it was as if the sky had fallen in. Maybe I was being insensitive but I think her fears were playing a big part too.

I can't remember the reason for our first real argument, but it played out calmly enough so no need for concern at that point. Over the next few years though, it became clear there was an unhealthy dynamic playing out on the occasions where we argued. She would claim that she was walking on eggshells not to upset me. But then having bottled up a load of stuff it would all come out in one go. For my part, I was reacting to what she was saying, becoming highly emotional and agitated in the process.

Over time, I developed a tactic of leaving the house to get some space and time to cool off before carrying on with further discussions.

In October 2012 Sue had a hysterectomy and her parents came to the house for 6 weeks to help with household chores so I could carry on working and having the children round. Sue struggled emotionally. When we went to a neighbour's party, she wanted to come home and I stayed for a bit longer. This was as if the sky had fallen in again. When we had some more counselling with Brian, I said Sue was jealous and controlling. This didn't help matters either.

On another occasion, we had a particularly severe row. Having pushed all of my buttons, I was in the mood to go and push some of hers so I went upstairs on the computer and searched for some group sex sites. Predictably, she went into orbit. And then she surprised me by clouting me across the cheek. I was fuming but didn't react in the moment, preferring instead to leave the house. I got into my car and drove off into the night.

I made it as far as Dawlish when I received a call from the police. They'd been called to the house and were concerned about Sue's safety and wanted me to return to the house immediately.

When I arrived back in the house, there were 2 police officers and I was given a hard time. I remember being completely confused seeing as it was me who had been hit. It occurred to me that Sue hadn't properly explained what had happened, so I pointed out to the police that she was the one who had hit me, not the other way around. They changed their tune sharply and offered me the chance to press charges. I declined to do so.

They were unwilling to just leave us on our own so we suggested phoning our best friend Ben, who came round straight away. Ben was as surprised as I was that the police had been involved, but Sue made the point that she was concerned for her safety. He stayed the night round at the house and all was well. I was still confused though as to how Sue could be scared of me when I considered myself to be a decent citizen. Little was I to know how all of my preconceptions about myself would be blown away in the later stages of bipolar disorder to come.

On another occasion, my impulsive behaviour had started to take hold. So as well as leaving the house, I was planning on driving for a long way in one direction or another before even considering coming back. I don't remember what we argued about, but I was so incensed that I got in the car and drove to London. My initial plan had been to drive all the way to Amsterdam via the channel tunnel, but I realised that I didn't have my passport with me so that put paid to that idea.

I stayed in a hotel in Sunbury-on-Thames, near the place I'd worked for a year after leaving school. I had some porn magazines with me, which were part of the argument. After enjoying them for a while, I made the decision that they were history so I put them all in the bin. I then phoned Sue and made peace with her before travelling back the next day.

When I arrived back in Exeter, she complained that I never did anything spontaneous with her. So we went on an instant long weekend break to St Ives in Cornwall. We stayed at a lovely hotel and I even bought Sue a fantastic silver feather necklace from a shop that was out of this world. It was made by North American Indians and Sue still wears it, even though she's now divorced from me. I remember thinking that this crazy impulsive behaviour was going to have to stop though because my spare funds were being depleted at a rate of knots. Of course I didn't realise at that stage that it would eventually lead to a very expensive divorce as well as a criminal conviction.

In the run-up to December 2013, Sue noticed that I was spending more and more time on my physics projects online. She was working away in London two days a week and then expecting that I would spend time with her when she returned. Whereas I was staying up until midnight and then waking up at 4am to send some more emails so my friends. This is a symptom of manic behaviour and according to Sue, I was pretty much back to the level I'd been with the Derren Brown incident.

I was also massaging my head a lot, which suggests I was suffering from headaches. And I'd been to the doctor a number of times and been prescribed Diazepam. None of this qualifies as a mental health diagnosis per se but it does show there were physical symptoms on the road to mania.

Mark Mansfield

Losing Touch With My Best Friend

Ben came into my life courtesy of Sue. He'd been a customer of her Bowen therapy business and was invited to our wedding party which I think was the first time I met him. Ben was good friends with Phil the policeman, also a customer of Sue's and was into Circling therapy.

Over the course of several months, Ben organised a number of Circling sessions which we all attended, along with some others too. A number of sessions were held in our lounge upstairs, by which time Sue and I were encouraging Ben to set it up as a business. I offered to do an introductory website, which I delivered with a minimum of hassle. Ben liked it and then ran with it himself using WordPress.

By this stage. Ben was running with me at lunchtimes down on the quay and I was really happy to have a best friend.

Then Ben met Beatrice at a Circling session in Amsterdam. This changed his priorities altogether. He did do a few public Circling sessions above the Evolution Cafe on Fore Street, Exeter. He also did some couples counselling on Queen Street which Sue and I took advantage of. As an aside, by this stage Sue and I had also had some traditional Relate counselling so we were able to judge the effectiveness of Ben's counselling and rated it very highly.

The Ben took the decision he wanted to move to Amsterdam as Beatrice was pregnant with their first baby. I was pleased for him but disappointed to be losing a friend. This was in the Summer.

Sue and I decided to visit Amsterdam in the Autumn. However, I made an absolutely stupid decision to eat a hash cake whole rather than take it easy. I had absolutely no idea how strong it was and my other experience smoking had been very mild so I was blind-sided by what came next. I basically passed out and then went wandering randomly through the streets. I ended up in hospital, the bill for which cost me a small fortune because I didn't have medical cover either. Later on that evening I was well enough to go back to their flat. I think Beatrice could have murdered me and I didn't blame her either.

Things were further strained in December when I was putting together my website www.healthy-service.org which included some references to Circling. Sue was horrified by some of what I'd said in the relationships section. Ben was equally horrified by my

34

increasingly un-Circling-like behaviour as he saw it and wanted to distance himself completely. For my part I was massively annoyed with both of them for not supporting me in what I was trying to do.

With the benefit of hindsight, these are all clear signs that a manic episode was taking hold. I'm particularly impressed with Ben's ability to spot that something was amiss even though he was in a different country at the time. Then the delusions and hallucinations started to happen.

I haven't been in contact with Ben since this time, which is a shame. Once the full effects of mania took over, my life had so many bizarre twists and turns that I wasn't capable of maintaining the relationship with him.

The Third Person In My Marriage

When I met Sue, she had been involved quite extensively with the Spiritualist Church and met a number of good friends. One of them, Steve, was the one who had recommended Bowen Therapy to her as a way of healing up from the back injury she'd sustained after slipping at work on an aircraft. Given that Sue had tried every other therapy under the Sun, to find one that worked was such a shock that she decided to train as a Bowen therapist herself and offer it to the general public. She was part-way through her training when I turned up on the scene.

Needless to say she had quite a lot of respect for Steve and I believe he had tried to enter a relationship with Sue, however, as he had been living with another lady Sue would not entertain the idea.

For his part, Steve clearly viewed Sue in the highest regard too and was giving the impression that he was a little hurt now I was there. He was still coming round to the house on a regular basis to discuss all things spiritual, which in his case went even beyond the level of spirituality Sue was prepared to entertain.

I remember Steve making some kind of threatening remark to me that if I ever hurt Sue I would have him to answer to. I didn't respond as I considered the possibility of that ever happening so remote that it wasn't worth considering. How naive I was.

Over the next few years, Steve remained as a good friend to Sue, including ongoing discussions online, after he'd moved out of the UK.

The circumstances under which he left the UK were quite amusing. Initially he'd decided to go motor-biking across Vietnam with some friends, as popularised by Top Gear. Sue told him to take extra money as he wouldn't be coming back! In the event, he stopped off in Cambodia on the way back and met a girl. By the time he got back to the UK, he realised that he didn't want to be here at all and wanted to go back to be with her. She was 28 and he was 49, or thereabouts.

I was sympathetic and decided to help. I offered to buy one of his Land Rovers off him as a way of freeing up his assets in the UK, given that they weren't selling. It was on the forecourt for 11k and I offered him 9k. With the benefit of hindsight, even this was probably too much, but it was at a time when I still had considerable reserves so I wasn't too concerned. How times have changed since then.

Steve was very grateful and left almost straight away to be with Sreyka and her son. Before long it was announced that she was pregnant and nine months later they named their baby Thomas George, after my son Thomas James. I was delighted.

After a while, the stormy times between Sue and me had started to be a regular thing. Rather annoyingly, Steve would start messaging Sue out of the blue at the exact same moment that something was going on.

I can't remember the circumstances or what we were arguing about, but I remember Sue saying that Steve was very angry and wanted to talk to me on the phone. At this point I put my foot down and objected. I said that it was like having a third person in our marriage, that whatever the argument was between Sue and me it was none of Steve's business. And why on Earth would I want to get on a phone call with someone who was openly angry in my direction?

The message got through and Steve backed down. Sue also acknowledged the point I had made and all was well. Little did any of us realise that things were about to flare up to such massive proportion that Steve's concerns were actually well-founded.

Mark Mansfield

The Force Was Staring Back At Me

My work as an amateur physicist began in 2009, towards the end of my first marriage. Prior to that I'd read a lot of magazines, watched episodes of the Sky At Night and doodled a lot in my notebook. So you could say that I was already an experienced armchair physicist. I made the decision to get out of the proverbial armchair and take a more active role. As a computer scientist by training and working in the computer industry during my day job, I'd spent a lot of time on the internet. I was keen to contribute something new that might be of use some day.

As luck would have it, I found www.artcompsci.org by Professors Piet Hut and Jun Makino. I was off, converting their gravitational simulation software from Ruby to C++. After making some enhancements and running a load of tests I built a website and even did a couple of lectures online and at Leiden University. You can see the results at www.grav-sim.com. It took 9 months to get that far.

By this stage, my curious side had started to take over. I plugged in some negative numbers just to see what would happen and was pleasantly surprised to find that my simulator didn't bat an eyelid. A universe full of negative mass was absolutely fine as far as it was concerned. As was an equal mix of positive and negative.

All of this was complete blasphemy as far as the standard model of physics is concerned, so you could say that my belief in negative mass counted as a delusion. It certainly put me in a stressful situation whenever I tried to discuss it with the people at Leiden, so I decided to take my wares elsewhere.

Claire decided to divorce me at that point, so that counts as a fairly major stressor. However, the prospect of meeting someone more compatible with me cheered me up and so I didn't go through an episode of mania at that point. In the event, I met Sue very quickly and she did a great job of reducing my stress levels.

Sue was also very good at encouraging me to take my alternative beliefs further. So I embarked on a second website where I explored the consequences of negative mass, along with a few other ideas I had. Note that the word "delusion" didn't come into it any more. By living with Sue and not associating with mainstream physicists, my alternative beliefs had no stress associated with them. So I found the courage to publish them on the public internet.

You can see the results at www.dirac-was-right.com. It took a couple of years to get to this point.

Within a few months I had some interesting feedback. One guy wanted me to do some work on the vacuum plasma thruster project. And some other guys were forming a group of like-minded alternative physicists on the internet, called The Mongols. So I had some real friends at last and I embarked on a series of in-depth discussions with them.

After a while, it became clear that my ideas on negative mass and the like were not going anywhere. The other Mongols didn't really buy into it in the way that I did, so I made the decision to get out of the armchair once more and find another physics project.

I homed in on the ionisation energies published on Wikipedia: https://en.wikipedia.org/wiki/Ionization_energies_of_the_elements_(data_page)

If I could find a way of accurately predicting the values from first principles, then this would count as a major contribution towards physics. I also had some tools I'd used in another project, something called Singular Value Decomposition, so I had everything I needed to get cracking.

About a month later, I had a working system. The accuracy was not really up to scratch, but that was something I could work on. All in all, I was feeling really good about myself. The ingredients for mania were falling into place.

3-12-2013:
I was staring at the results from my ionisation energy calculator and I thought I could see a pattern. In itself, this was nothing too surprising because there are at least 3 levels of pattern in the data known from electron quantum numbers. However, an additional pattern could mean the missing link for getting the additional level of accuracy that I so badly needed.

At that moment in time, my belief system underwent a significant change because I thought I had found a new way of looking at the atom itself. And with that, I saw a flash of light as if it had come from the centre of the Earth. And the rumbling sound of an explosion too. I was stupefied.

It reminded me of the first time I was done by a speeding camera. I'd noticed a flash from behind, looked in my rear view mirror and then took the second flash directly to my eyeballs. Only that was two flashes rather than one.

With the benefit of hindsight, you could say that my belief was a delusion. And you could certainly say that what I'd seen was a hallucination because there were no speed cameras near my computer desk. However, this was before I'd been diagnosed with bipolar disorder so as far as I was concerned, these things were real.

This started to trigger all sorts of alternative beliefs in my mind and that the force was literally unravelling in front of my eyes. As the dream of many physicists is to come up with a unified theory that combines everything, it was natural that I would think in terms of a "unified force". If pushed, I would choose electromagnetism as the most likely candidate and when referring to it as "the force" I would think of Star Wars.

At this point, I thought I was completely sane and healthy. I had absolutely no idea that these alternative beliefs would propel me through a truly bizarre series of further manic episodes.

One of the first things I did was to announce my discovery on my website. I didn't refer to the flash of light as such, but nevertheless wrote the following.

7-12-2013:
I am a scientist.

In 1992, I graduated from Churchill College, Cambridge, having studied physics in the first year and computer science in the final 2 years.

The last 20 years have been spent in the software industry, 10 years as a C++ developer and 10 years as a project manager.

Since 2009, I have spent many evenings and weekends working on physics projects.

On 7th September 2013, I was contacted by Theofanes. He said "I've got a great bunch going with Kingsley and Henning".

We talked a lot about physics.

On 3rd December 2013 I made what I consider to be a scientific discovery.

On 7th December 2013 Kingsley finally took an interest in looking at the results.

I had to send a couple of professors his way first to take an interest in his dream to solve the QED puzzle.
Up until this time, computer science had not been considered a viable way of doing an experiment.

The data is the atomic ionisation data that is publicly available on Wikipedia.

The method is to use a Singular Value Decomposition to find coefficients for a linear sequence of non-linear terms.

The result is a 5th order power series, with some extra stuff to represent the quantum numbers.

The result is expressed in PHP code format. Science has never been done this way before.

My conclusions are that the potential surrounding the atomic nucleus is approximately Coulomb. It's 99% based on the Z^2 component.

Henning has taken the role of ace blogger for the group. He has recently upgraded to wiki format.

Theo is seeking the truth. He has yet to grasp that we have actually found something. I am hoping Kinglsey will persuade him otherwise.

John joined the group recently. I am hoping he finds the time to follow his physics dreams and join us in studying this problem.

We fly under the banner "Mongol Physics"

Henning is publishing under the banner "Mongol Media"

I have sent my results to Kaggle who are the world leader in running data analysis competitions.

The response from Angus was very positive:

Mark, thanks for getting in touch and apologies for the delay responding! This sounds like a super-interesting problem, subject to the obvious concern of participants submitting the ground truth as a submission (which we've dealt with in the past for Getting Started competitions like the Titanic one). However, we don't have any meaningful way of scoring the complexity of the submitted solution, which makes me concerned that this doesn't quite fit the model for the Kaggle platform - given the relatively small size of the dataset, I fear that the majority of submissions would be way overfitted to the exact values of the observed data without necessarily adding anything to the understanding or extendibility of the predictions outside the set. What do you think?

I have responded to him, explaining to him that what we are doing is science. Working with real data and building a theory. According to Occam's razor, the simplest theory that fits the facts is best. I'm sure Kaggle will make improvements.

To date we are accurate for Hydrogen-like and Helium-like ions only.

We need more talented people to respond to the challenge of making it work for Lithium et al.

I could have started with the spectral data - that is my next challenge.

Mark Mansfield - 7th December 2013

The Mongol Song

The first written evidence I can find of my increasingly manic behaviour is the following piece I wrote about my Mongol friends. Complete with megalomania. It was the first song I'd written in my entire life (and probably the last).

9-12-2013:

We are the Mongols.
I am the Wild Man.
We will take the whole fucking world by storm.
We are the Mongols.
I am the Front Man.
We will teach the whole world our song.
We are the Mongols.
I am Genghis Khan.

With all due respect, please would that fucking Wild Man piss off out of my fucking territory.

We are the Mongols.
I am the Wise Man.

Please would you guys stop pissing about ... I can't hear myself think!

Reconnection Therapy

I've already mentioned a number of therapies I've received over the years. The concise list is as follows:

1.   Cognitive Behavioural Therapy, courtesy of the NHS
2.   Singles and Couples Counselling, courtesy of Relate
3.   Bowen Therapy, courtesy of Sue and Jean
4.   Circling, courtesy of Ben
5.   Shamanistic Healing, courtesy of Steve
6.   The Reconnection, courtesy of Sue

Of all the therapies, the most dramatic effect came from The Reconnection. Billed as a method to bring you in touch with your true self, it certainly did that for me by helping to send me on my bipolar / manic trip.

I wrote about my thoughts on some of this in the following emails.
Flight 666 To Mongol Slavery, 10-12-2013:

Mongols: 1
Future Mongols: Please let's keep this as low as possible
Banner: Psychology
Basis: Language
Direction: Bad Faith
Seeking: Mind Control

This is where I think the risk with Circling lies.

Ben believes in Enlightenment (as I do).

I don't think he sees the associated risk / connection with Mind Control. (unlike me).

I believe Beatrice may be a victim of this and Ben has yet to realise.

Or maybe he does realise and he's looking after her. I don't know.

Apologies for the extreme sensitivity of this.

Ben's path took him via Sue and I before he moved out to Amsterdam.

Beatrice's path was via a different group, in Amsterdam before she met Ben.

Note I have not cc'd Theo on this because I think he is the least strong member of the Mongol group in psychological terms.

I really don't know where to take this one next.

Help from a professor of psychology might be a good start.

Can you guys recommend anyone?
Please, I need help here.

Personality Types, 13-12-2013:

My preferred starting point is the Wisdom of the Enneagram.

This is not to say that this book is any better or worse than any of the other books out there.

Just that it is the one I am most familiar with.

I buy into it a lot.

It was recommended to me by Ben.

As far as I can tell:

- I am type 5, The Investigator
- Sue is type 8, the Challenger
- Ben is type 2, the Helper
- Beatrice is type 1, the Reformer

The idea is that each of us is pre-programmed (either genetically or by the circumstances of our childhood), to follow one of these paths.

Once we're on a path, there is little we can do to get off that path ... we just need to follow it to its logical conclusion. Our individual route to "Enlightenment".

The concept of personal development is then introduced on a scale of 1 to 10.

Levels 1-3 are "unhealthy"
Levels 4-7 are "normal"
Levels 8-10 are "healthy"

Maybe those are not the best words, but they'll do for now.

People at level 1 are likely to be in jail.

Level 2 out in the community but known to the police.

Level 3 kind of get by but can be unpleasant to deal with, like the idiot who has the allotment next to Sue and I in Pinces Allotments, St Thomas.

In general terms, we expect children to go through these levels at school. Fights in the playground are all part and parcel of finding out what it is like to behave in these ways. Some kids decide to take the "good" path and go further up the scale. Others either stay where they are or descend back to lower levels.

In everyday life, most people are in the 4-7 range. The best way of getting through this lots seems to be a large dose of life experiences, learning off each other.

That said, it can be helpful if a wife or husband has a personality type that brings solutions to the problems the other one is having. This is what has happened to me and Sue. It works both ways ... she has taught me as much as I have taught her.

Getting from level 8 upwards is difficult.

My take is that the Circling offered by Ben is a useful technique in getting up to level 9. However, you won't get that far unless you are already at level 7 or 8 to begin with.

My take is also that The Reconnection offered by Eric Pearl is a way of getting from level 9 to level 10.

However, I have a real problem with what Eric Pearl is doing for 2 reasons.

1. He takes personal details of everyone who has had it and could be passing them on to the mind control bunch.

2. He is practising it on children who may only be at level 3 or 4. This has the effect of making the children very suggestible and open to manipulation to others.

Have any of you seen Derren Brown? You'll know about triggers that are used for hypnotherapy.

The trigger for Eric Pearl's "The Reconnection" is the number 333. It is the cost that he demands must be taken as the payment.

I make the observation that 333 is precisely half of 666 and relate that back to my previous email regarding Flight 666 To Mongol Slavery.

It may be the case that Eric Pearl himself is unaware of what he is doing.

The Reconnective Healing aspect of what he sells is the nice warm fluffy exterior that draws people in and may well have a healing benefit (not sure on that one).

The Reconnection is the bit that seems to have a dramatic effect. It's to do with the psychology of letting go of money, sending the payment to the "gypsy" who allegedly set this whole thing up.

My take is that the gypsy is associated with the mind control bunch.

So, if what Eric Pearl is doing has a lovely exterior but a nasty interior, we need to do precisely the opposite.

We need to go in with a nasty exterior, so they don't suspect us. Backed up by a lovely interior which relates to the good faith of our true intentions.

Ben personifies this approach. He refuses to accept he's a type 2, preferring to think of himself as Type 8 which has the hard exterior. That said, he is a marine and I wouldn't mess with him.

He has also spent several months at sea defending from Somali pirates and the like.

I hope you guys can start to see where I'm coming from with this.

Planted Messages

By this time, I was starting to believe that messages coming my way from various places were significant and intended for me. The first documentary evidence I have of this is from some emails that I sent to myself, noting my thoughts.

15-12-2013:
And on the subject of planted messages, can I assume that:

- The woman who turned up at one of our neighbour's parties, purporting to be a friend of Miccy and Chrissy, was on a mission to promote Bowen therapy to the UK? She suggested I started blogging messages back to Australia and in effect, that is what I have done recently via Kingsley and John

- The phrase "Derren Brown is Evil" was planted with Sue's father's brother when I met him in Portugal. That one had a particularly deep effect on me, putting me into a very withdrawn state while I went through a process of deciding how much of anything I actually trusted, including everyone around me.

- The phrase "Quantum Chemistry Industry" was planted by Kingsley ... again that one had a very deep effect on me, prompting me to apply the SVD method (which was a tool I carried with me from my Cambridge days) to the ionisation data. I doubt that any of you knew that was a skill I had though. Jonathan passed on the word about that one ... and I first used it to have a go at grey-hound racing (with little success I might add).

- The phrase DNA test was somehow passed on to Sue. Again that one had a very deep effect, while I figured out what on Earth I thought about all of that. This would appear to be the most contentious topic of all ... with everyone coming at me with pitch-forks whenever I bring it up in conversation.

- That the wake up calls via loud noises from motorbikes zooming around, industry from Marsh Barton etc. are basically you guys trying to tell me I should get out of bed?

- It is definitely the case that I am at my most creative / talkative / full of ideas when I have just woken up.

Last xmas I gave you my heart.
But the very next day you gave it away.
This year, to save me from tears

I'll give it to someone special

Love to you all :-)

Mark xxxxxxxxxxxxxxxxxxxxxxxxxxxx

16-12-2013:

Mayfair sounds nice. Am sure Sue would love that too :-)

Not sure about the meaning of NUFC cancelling (part of) my order? Either way, I'll be wearing my Newcastle shirt today.

The Meetup calendar gets a "Blimey" :-)

The last I heard I was taking my daughter to school this morning so getting to Okehampton for 9am may be a little tricky.

I can float the idea with Sue though. She still has a commitment to her Bowen customers though ...

17-03-2013:

The Police Greatest Hits.

Love them :-)

Want to get my son up to Newcastle on 2nd and 3rd for introductory training. His mum agrees. But you guys have apparently passed some law that says I'm not allowed to take children out of school for any reason.

WTF am I supposed to do??

Bought Nelson Mandela's book - The Heart of a Rainbow Nation. What he did surpasses anything else.

And Virgin can piss off with their threatening "late payment" and "legal action" messages.

They make more than enough money out of me and I've just paid them 400 quid so what exactly is their problem???

The total outstanding balance is 193 quid and they want to ruin my credit rating ...

I hope they have a nice party on the 12 quid late payment charge.

FFS

Remember to phone the headmaster regarding the trip to Newcastle on 2nd and 3rd Jan.

Or not as the case might be ... Kings of Leon trumps that one. Thanks guys.

On the subject of my brother.

Sue and I got married in St Lucia, taking just our 5 children along with us.

We organised a wedding party at our house on our return to the UK. Friends and family only (many of them were neighbours from Sanford Place). We did not invite my mother or my father because we were both profoundly uncomfortable with the way they were behaving towards us leading up to the wedding.

I did invite my brother because he had been behaving completely reasonably up until this point.

After a few beers and after the children had left, Paul and I struck up a conversation. He was openly abusive to my face, in front of all of my guests. I then challenged him with what he had just said. He denied saying it ... this was only 5 seconds later. Classic abusive behaviour.

If you want witnesses to any of this, you can ask:

- Phil the policeman
- Ben the marine
- Dave the fireman
- Patrick the accountant
- My wife Sue the Bowen therapist

I escorted Paul out of the premises. He will tell you that he left of his own volition.

At Christmas time, my mother attempted to organise an event at Sanford Place. She insisted that my brother come along. I told her there was no way he was welcome in my house. She refused to accept my story.

My brother phoned me and I explained what I thought of his behaviour.

He said I was a fucking pathetic twat.

I told him to fuck off.

That was the last I heard from him.

On the subject of guns.

I have an air-rifle in my shed. It was a present to my son on his birthday and we have only ever used it to shoot pellets at a paper / metal target at the end of our garden.

My father thinks the intention of the gun is for me to shoot him.

The only person with any real guns is my brother. He has several locked away in his basement along with goodness knows how much ammunition, tins of tuna etc.

I can only hope that if my brother does ever intend to use his guns on anyone, that he blows himself up without harming anyone else. I thought this sort of thing was only supposed to happen in Texas.

Go figure.

And while I think of it, the person I would most like to meet right now is Norbert Singer.

Superseded by my eldest daughter, but only if that is what she wants to. Hugs all round.

Freedom of Expression

The subject of Top Woman first arose in the following email. It would take over a year before I found her.

18-12-2013:

That's absolutely fine sweetie, no worries.

In all likelihood, it will be just me and the kids going.

The physics guys will probably decline on the grounds of the flight costs. Although they like to "talk the talk", I don't think any of them are currently up to "walking the walk", with the possible exception of Henning who did step up to the mark by pledging $1000 towards my "Competition to Make a Scientific Breakthrough". That particular project will probably remain on the launch-pad because Kingsley has just started to get going big-time with his Maxwell-Dirac investigations. I am trying to support him as much as I can because I believe in what he is doing. So his project is currently taking the highest priority in physics land.

The First Mongol Convention will most likely remain a fantasy until such times as I can find a sponsor to pay for all of the expenses.

And as to whether any of the friends-and-neighbours or Ben want to get involved, well that's up to them.

You and Ben will need to start to think seriously about how you're going to promote your project. I appreciate that NUFC may not be the most obvious choice for that. However, it does really suit my freedom-of-expression quest, which is also something I truly believe in (and a natural consequence of Circling).

I appreciate that you find my proposed slogan offensive. I need you to appreciate that one of the main reasons I am doing it is to provoke discussion, particularly from women on the subject of swear-words, which get used a lot in business / professional contexts, behind closed doors.

My thesis is that freedom-of-expression is the main reason that women don't get promoted to the top levels of management.

Margaret Thatcher and Angela Merkel being clear exceptions.

Clearly we can't ask Baroness Thatcher to comment on any of this, but Angela Merkel is a clear contender for Top Woman in the world right now.

My slogan is:

This is who
I AM
Who the f***
ARE YOU?

This is all about identity and freedom of expression. Things we have lost in the modern world. Things that Game of Thrones has in spades, which is why we all love that series.

I want that slogan on the back of my NUFC shirt, as long as NUFC themselves are in agreement with all of this.

Their fan's song "We are the Geordies" is a natural fit for my status as a complete nutter on the physics front and all other things too.

It also speaks to my own mental health history.

I like NUFC a lot.

My son chose them.

He chose well.

The Birds Were Mine

21-12-2013:

I had decided to run the Parkrun at Killerton on a Saturday morning. Whilst generally out running at lunchtimes, I had noticed birds flying past me in the same direction as I was going. So the general thought of birds reacting to me was already in my head.

When I got to the event, I was pretty much the first runner to turn up. Speaking to the organiser, he said something like this will be the first of many and gave me a knowing look. I took this to mean I would be running lots of Park runs in future in an effort to win a T-shirt.

I walked up to the starting line, knowing that I was at half an hour ahead of time. The birds in the trees overhead were going berserk with the amount of noise they were making and flying from tree to tree. I gazed upwards with a real sense that they were reacting to me and my unified force / electromagnetic field effect. When I waved my arms, they seemed to redouble their efforts and made even more noise.

Felt great at the start line, but going too soft and slipped at the first hurdle. Expended way too much energy skating the first mile and had nothing left for the finish. Will trade my horse-shoes for spikes next time. Also beginning to think the sugar in the Lucozade Sport didn't help me this morning. So will trade that for water next time.

Hats off to the Kenyan chap who blew everyone away this morning! At least we were all assuming he was from somewhere in North Africa. His presence was electrifying.

Message To Dana Scully (a.k.a. Richard Dawkins)

In response to an article about Richard Dawkins in New Scientist, I sent the following email from me to me, in the hope it would get through to him.

24-12-2013:
Dear Dana,
I believe.
I believe in the human spirit.
I also believe in the power of the human mind to cure many of the ailments that plague today's society.
I also believe in the power of healthy relationships between humans (and possibly animals too) to help solve their problems too.
You may take this as meaning I am a spiritualist.
Actually I don't much care for the activities that go on in the local spiritualist church.
Neither does my wife Sue, although she is more of a spiritualist than me. It's the political in-fighting and power-play that are common to many religious institutions that she doesn't care for.
For people who are of even more spiritualist nature than Sue or I, I refer to Sue's friend Mary who we are hoping will offer her services as part of the St Thomas / Loft Club / Holistic Healing Centre being proposed by Sue. I also refer to Steve who can be found leading shamanistic practises in Cambodia. He has treated many celebrities.
I am a scientist.
I qualified in computer science at Churchill College, Cambridge in 1992. This included a first year in natural sciences.
I appreciate that computer science is not regarded as "science" by academia. This is because it is not an academic discipline. It is an industrial discipline. This is why nobody reads computer science journals.
For my industrial credentials, I submit my CV.
For my recent achievements in science I present a sequence of 3 websites:
1. The boundary between computer science and standard gravitational physics is represented by www.grav-sim.com. For referees, please refer to professors:
- Piet Hut
- Peter Teuben
- Simon Portegies-Zwart.
I also did a sequence of online presentations at the Meta-Institute of Computational Astrophysics and a real-world presentation at the initial AMUSE "Star Trek" conference at Leiden University.

2. The boundary between standard and alternative physics is represented by www.dirac-was-right.com. For referees, please refer to my online physics companions "The Mongols":
- Theofanes
- Henning
- Kingsley
- John
They have their own website under construction www.mongolphysics.com

3. The boundary between science and the human spirit is represented by my new website, under-construction www.healthy-service.org. Perhaps psychology is the best description for this. Referees as per the discussion above. The main purpose of this effort is to assist the NHS in taking delivery of the miraculous Bowen therapy developed by Tom Bowen in Australia.

I also have made some recent progress on the marketing front, via my proposed "Competition to Make a Scientific Breakthrough" with www.kaggle.com. This project is on the launch pad, pending sponsors. You may also refer to my previous email trail "Flight 9137 To Mongol Mania".

I hope my messages get through.

Kind Regards,

Fox Mulder

Insanity In Weston Super Mare

In the run up to Christmas 2013 I remained convinced that I'd made a scientific discovery.

There were a number of other things going on in my private life, which distracted me from the physics. I put my creative energy into building another website www.healthy-service.org, no longer available unfortunately. It presented:

- Bowen Therapy, which is my ex-wife Sue's business, www.sue-mansfield.com
- Shamanistic Healing, which is my friend Steve's business, www.steve-jeanes.com
- Circling, which is my friend Ben's business
- My own ideas on Identity and Relationships

The level of emotion that went into producing that site was huge. it drew together strands of thought from many directions and put them together into one framework. So much so that it fuelled my manic behaviour and led me into conflict with Sue, Ben and Steve.

Christmas itself went OK, though according to Sue I just "wasn't there". We had the children round, both hers and mine, with the exception of my eldest daughter who was opting out of anything to do with me. This had hurt me greatly earlier in the year, but I thought I'd got on top of it. Famous last words.

I remember the kids making a comment like it was a live-in psychological experiment. That tallies with the general sense of mania I'd been experiencing without knowing what it was. And also gives you an idea of what conversation topics tended to be like between Sue and myself.

On Boxing day, we headed out to my place of work, where Sue had the cleaning contract. My kids came with us. We were all in a grumpy mood, but I had no idea of how explosive the situation was. My son sparked it off by taking the 5-a-side football and starting to kick it around the office. I told him off. But to my horror, Sue had a very loud and direct go at him too. I went into orbit. We'd discussed this type of thing years ago and Sue had sold me on a book that said parenting had to be done by the parent, so I was horrified to see her doing the exact opposite.

When we got home, my son locked himself in his room and even my youngest daughter went on hunger strike. Having lost the relationship with my eldest daughter, I was alarmed to the core to see a similar situation happing with my other 2 children. In reality, the children cooled off quite quickly, but in my mind this was the end of the world and I just couldn't calm down.

I went for a walk round the block to consider what had happened and went past a lady on the street who was saying to her friend "she's a f***ing c*** that one". In my delusional state, I thought she was talking about Sue and I wasn't going to argue with the sentiments, though I can now see I was being unreasonable. I went back to the house and had an all-out row with Sue. I smashed the crockery sat on the draining board, took my passport, booked a holiday on the internet and stormed out of the house. I even left my 2 children in her care without telling my first wife.

I had intended to drive to Bristol Airport but as I didn't need to be there until the next day, I took a left and went to Weston Super Mare instead. In the event I stayed there for a couple days, so I never got to go on holiday after all. Wasting money on crazy purchases like that is a typical symptom of mania.

I parked in the car park of the Grand Atlantic Hotel and went inside. They were full, as it was the Christmas period. So I walked down the sea front to the Premier Inn where they had a room spare, despite also being very busy. I chose to leave my car at the Grand Atlantic.

Believe it or not I was feeling quite good about myself. Although I'd fallen out with Sue in a major way, I was full of the thought that my daily activities, websites and emails were all being observed by government agents and that I'd really discovered something with my physics.

I stayed in my room until the evening and then went for a walk. After taking a couple of turns to the left, I came to a night club with a group of young people waiting outside. I thought the bouncers were beckoning me to come inside, presumably to find a new partner for the night given the situation with Sue. To my credit, I declined this particular offer, preferring to keep myself to myself instead.

I kept walking and after several twists and turns, came across a Batman mural in one of the side streets. I thought this was freshly painted in my honour and I took the super-hero sentiment as a huge compliment and boost to my already inflated ego.

When I got to the sea front, I turned left and headed back to the hotel.

I needed a charger for my Samsung Galaxy S4 phone so I asked the receptionist. She didn't have one but said she would ask around.

In the morning, after breakfast, the receptionist was there again and she offered me an Android phone charger. She said it belonged to the chef but he was happy to lend it to me. I was delighted and said thank-you.

I took it to my room, plugged it in and kept it powered on just long enough to send some messages.

Back in the lobby, I decided that my phone had too many high-energy messages stored and was giving away my position too easily. So I offered it to the receptionist and asked if she could give it to the chef. It was my way of saying thank-you for the charger, that he should get a free phone. I found out later that she put it in the safe instead because she though my gesture was particularly weird.

I then walked off into town. First stop was an electrical shop where I asked about mobile phones. The shop assistant gave me directions to a phone shop. I then thought about it and decided I would get a new one from work, so I said to the shop assistant I would be OK. He said "are you sure" and I remember thinking this was the government talking to me.

After that I went into Marks & Spencer where a child was doing a Nazi-style goose-step, presumably in protest to the woman looking after her. I didn't see it that way though and took it as a comment about me personally. It made me feel quite uncomfortable.

Then I walked into Mountain Warehouse and for some reason was fascinated by the socks they had on offer.

By mid-morning I was in a cafe enjoying a cup of hot chocolate, watching the other customers getting on with their lives. At this point I wasn't really sure what I was doing so I decided to do some sight-seeing by going down to the pier.

A number of men came out of the amusement arcade along the way and started cheering. I thought they were responding to me, but I kept my head down and carried on.

At the pier, I walked down one side all the way to the far end, where I was prevented from going any further by a metal gate. My head was full of lines of force and I imagined that one day I would be able to go all the way down the pier with greater effect on the world around me. I walked back to the middle then round to the other side, where it was the same story.

When I got back to the middle, a couple of seagulls were flying overhead, holding their position because of the stiff breeze. I thought they were there just to see me and I gesticulated at them, waving my arms, cheering and clapping.

At that point I heard a ship sound its horn and I turned around to look. Then cars started beeping their horns and cheering erupted along the seafront. I am tempted to think that all of this was a hallucination, but it fitted in with my delusions of grandeur so I didn't question it at the time.

I'm not sure what I did for lunch but I can remember going back to the hotel lobby and asking for directions to an internet cafe. The receptionist gave me a verbal description of the route and off I went.

As I got towards the area of town I'd been before I took a wrong turn. Then managed to follow a street back to the right place and picked up the route once more. Then I walked right past the internet cafe and got to the end of that street before I realised I'd gone too far. A woman came out of a door and walked back up the street in the direction I was looking to go. I thought she was a government agent showing me the way.

Back at the internet cafe, it was closed. On the door it said "Something Special" and I imagined that it was like something out of James Bond.

So I headed back up the street until the next shop which caught my eye, which said "Little Witch" or something like that. It was a shop full of tarot cards and alternative therapy promotions and that sort of thing. Again I thought James Bond.

Then I turned around and gentleman with a hat was outside the pub opposite smoking a cigarette. By now I was convinced that he was a government agent, so I went inside, ordered a cider and sat down.

I watched TV and listened to the conversations at the bar. It seemed to me that the gentleman on the end of the bar was a spy. When he got up to leave, he adjusted the newspaper in his coat pocket, which I interpreted as meaning that I should get a copy and take a look.

When I did manage to get hold of a copy of the paper, I saw a full page advert for Mountain Warehouse where the character Bob had climbed a mountain and was on top of the world. Given that Bob is a pseudo-name I had used on a few occasions, all of this seemed like a scary reference to me and my activities that morning. I'm sure now that it was all just a coincidence, but at the time it was all way too spooky and helped my delusions to continue.

When I got back to the hotel, the receptionist queried whether I really wanted to give my phone to the chef and I said yes.

I then checked out and walked back to the Grand Atlantic to get my car. The car park was empty and so was the hotel. I thought there had been a bomb scare or something like that. It didn't occur to me that maybe the hotel was giving its staff some time off. I was really spooked and drove around Weston Super Mare for a bit before I decided it was safe to be on my way.

I headed back to my place of work in Exeter, having had probably the craziest set of experiences I'd ever had in my life, though they all seemed very real at the time.

The Police Took My Front Door Key

Although things had been rocky in the run-up to Christmas 2013, nothing could have prepared me for what happened soon after. To this day I remain astounded that I behaved as I did and even writing it down leaves me with a sense of trepidation.

When I returned from Weston Super-Mare I went to my place of work. There was a notice on the railings outside the theatre that said "Home". I thought this meant that work was now home and they were welcoming me. Once at work, I used the internet to check on some things and decided I'd better find another hotel.

So I went to Exmouth. On the way past Dart's Farm I saw their sign which basically said "Vegetables, who grew yours?" I thought they were referring to the size of my testicles.

At Exmouth I pulled up in the Bay Grand Hotel car park on the sea front and then realised that the hotel was closed. I parked in a reserved zone but as I was a VIP guest on planet Earth I thought that it would be OK for me to leave it there.

I ran down the seafront looking for another hotel, feeling like I was a fugitive on the run and that people were out to get me. I saw the Ashton Court Hotel up the hill on the left, ran up to it and found that it was closed too. At that point I didn't know what to do so I turned around and walked across the road. There was a man there who was seemingly making a fuss about reading his newspaper. With that he folded the paper away and walked off. Given my experience in the pub in Weston, I was convinced this was a clear sign that I should follow this man.

So I then embarked on what turned out to be a bit of a wild goose chase. I followed the man until he went through a locked gate and inside a house. At that point there were 2 women walking with a pushchair, so I thought that I was supposed to follow them. This carried on with me following several other people, until eventually I got back to Ashton Court. I was bewildered, but I looked the other way down the street and saw the sign for The Royal Beacon Hotel. Finally, I had found somewhere that was open. I booked into room 202.

I stayed there for a few days, intending this to be my holiday before I figured out what I was doing next. During this time, I went swimming at Exmouth pool and took the train back up to Exeter so I could use the internet at work once again. As I went through the ticket gate at Exeter Central, I noticed a tiny yellow sticker on my ticket with the number 202 written on it. This terrified me into thinking that even the station staff were government agents who knew what I was doing. This particular coincidence seems so unlikely that I wonder whether it was a hallucination.

Outside the station, an advert for First Great Western included Elsie and her grandchildren. Elsie was the name of my grandmother, who had died a few years previously. My head was in a spin.

Later on when I got back to the hotel, I recovered my car and removed the yellow 202 sticker from my ticket. If this was a hallucination, it was a seriously good one.

Later that evening, the light from down the street lit up the side wall making it look like a rocket ship for a trip to Mars.

Apparently at this point I went home. I don't recall what happened, but Sue reckons I was there for a few days before another argument caused me to blow up with my emotions. This time I collected a few things and packed the car. Then I smashed several pictures, with the glass shattering down the stairs. Sue made the comment that at this rate we would be seeking mediation and not counselling. I clearly had deaf ears at that point because I just stormed out of the house.

Back at the hotel in Exmouth again, I organised all of my possessions around the room in a kind of shrine. Things like books, magazines and my chess set which was in the back of my car. At this point the craziest of thoughts were going through my head as I was broadcasting a message to the universe about how I felt about all these things.

It was at this point that the police turned up and took my front door key from me. At the time I agreed this was a good idea, though with hindsight I think I should have exercised my right to hang onto it. Clearly Sue was scared about me returning to the house, mainly based on the smashed picture experience. Having largely calmed down, I was inclined to be sympathetic. What I didn't realise was there was no process for getting my key back, so I was effectively signing up to be a homeless person when the money for hotels ran out. The stress associated with that situation was what fuelled the next round of crazy behaviour and I have to say I blame the police for that.

Prior to Christmas, I had booked a couple's counselling session with Relate. Given the overall situation, I thought that was a good venue to talk things through with Sue. So I turned up in Tiverton at the allotted time. This was only to find that Sue declined to turn up at all. I was shocked. She hadn't even notified me that she wouldn't be there, which was unlike her. So I had no chance to postpone or rearrange the session, I had to go through with it. And pay for a couple's session even though only one of us was turning up.

To my credit, I didn't get angry at any of this and had a measured discussion with Brian the counsellor. I basically told him that I wanted my front door key back, but was clearly faced with a situation where that wasn't going to happen. I later found out that Sue had been advised by the police not to turn up for the counselling session.

I went back to my place of work where I could use the internet. By this stage, the anger had taken hold and I did a couple of things that I truly regret. Firstly, I wrote some absolutely awful, horrid emails to Sue, reprinted in the next section. In my mind I was blaming her too for making me homeless, so I didn't hold back and I told her exactly what I thought of her and her behaviour. Then I went to her website, which had been developed by me, and changed the homepage to "Sue Mansfield, F***ing C***" or something like that.

No sooner had I done that then when 2 policemen arrived in the office. One of them was on the phone, receiving a message about Stumbleupon reporting offensive language on Sue's website. It was only there for a few minutes and I replaced the homepage straight away. We talked about the offensive email. They made the point that they were concerned about my behaviour and mental state. I agreed to go with them to the hospital to be checked out, as well as explaining all the things that were bothering me about the current situation.

I attended the hospital and then found that although the police were keen to escort me there, I would be finding my own way back. So I walked.

I later heard that I'd basically killed Sue with my offensive emails. She was hurt to the core, which shows that she still wanted to be in a relationship with me at that point. The trouble was that together with the police she'd taken my front door key off me, refused to attend counselling and was refusing to talk to me about any of this.

So the only conclusion I could come to was that the relationship was over.

To conserve money, I moved out of the hotel in Exmouth and moved in to the Globe Backpackers Hotel which was just around the corner from my work. I would be staying in a shared dormitory, but at least it was cheap as chips. It was then that I did a third thing that I truly regret. Even though I was still in love with Sue and desperately wanted to get our relationship back together, I made an impulsive decision to make the best of a bad situation and have an affair.

In the dormitory, I was bragging about having lined up a date with a lady in Plymouth. Little did I know that one of the others would report this to the owner, who in turn reported it to his wife, who in turn was friends with Sue. Apparently Sue was both mortally wounded to hear that I was having an affair, as well as really cross with her friend for seemingly gloating in the situation.

The affair lasted for a few weeks, by which time I managed to re-establish email contact with Sue. Of course by this stage the damage had been done and although Sue and I got back together for another year after this, she claims to this day that she hasn't healed up from what happened. I am truly sorry for the things I did. Though equally I maintain that what the police did in making me homeless added rocket fuel to an already flammable situation.

I remain shocked that the police offered no way of me getting my front door key back. When all is said and done, the house was owned 50% by each of us so it belonged to me. To just take it and leave me homeless was wrong.

Toxic Emails

I am absolutely ashamed that I ever sent these awful emails. I love Sue but had temporarily lost sight of this due to my anger and my manic behaviour. The easiest way forward would be for me not to print them, but I have decided to do so in an effort to show the extreme emotional state I was in.

The fact that I can go from terrifying abuse like this back to a normal loving relationship is why I question whether I might have Borderline Personality Disorder as well as bipolar. Please send answers on a postcard. And no wonder that Sue has divorced me, although that didn't happen until a year later and more abuse.

Date: Sat, 28 Dec 2013 10:42:14 Mark Mansfield wrote:
Dear Susan,
I will be filing for divorce on grounds of unreasonable behaviour (yours).
I will cite the incident that was lodged with the police 9 months as evidence. No doubt there will be an ongoing discussion about what has gone on in relation to my daughter, last year and with my son, in the recent incident. Your continued policy of putting yourself first above all others and in all situations, regardless of whether there are children involved, has landed you in this mess.
When all is said and done, I only stand for 2 things on the domestic front:
1. Against cheating
2. Against bullying
You were guilty of the first point in your previous marriage.
You're guilty of the second point to this very day, in spite of repeated warnings.
Ben was right ... you've learned absolutely nothing from circling. This is because you have no intention of ever changing.
You will not be seeing any of my children again. Most likely neither will your children, although they are welcome to do as they see fit and I see them as good people too.
I will still have to come and go via the house in order to continue my life, such as it is.
If you really want to know how I feel ...
You are the Fucking Cunt.
You are the Destroyer of Relationships.
Your Bowen business is a Bully Factory in disguise.
I hope you Burn in Hell.
The Hotter the Better.
The Sooner the Better.

Your love is worth nothing more to me than a power-grabbing sham.

Happiness for me lies with a better woman, if I can find one and she'll have me.

God alone knows what's in store for you.

Kind Regards,

Mark

Date: Sun, 29 Dec 2013 09:44:39, Mark Mansfield wrote:

Dear Patsy,

I realise that we have had a "Bit of a Barney" recently.

I have a meal ticket courtesy of my company.

Would you care to come to dinner with me at the Thai Orchid?

I will need to pop home for a change of clothes first.

Have been on a bit of a mission and am still in the same clothes I left the house in.

Am still on a mission actually.

I would like to donate the entire contents of my / our safe to the homeless charity Emmaus.

This is in response to their "I am a Piece of Paper" leaflet, which says it all as far as I'm concerned.

I am sure they will do a better job of auctioning off the contents than either you or I would do.

When all is said and done, they have more time on their hands than you or I.

They are also in more need of the funds than you or I at this point in time.

We're trading on thin air from here on.

It's called Goodwill.

Kind Regards,

Bob

On 29 December 2013 10:32:00, Mark Mansfield wrote:

OK, whatever.

I'm off to commit suicide.

Mark

Date: Sun, 29 Dec 2013 10:36:57, Mark Mansfield wrote:

May as well get there first before any other angry person with a vengeance really does try to kill me off.

Mark

Date: Sun, 29 Dec 2013 13:23:00, Mark Mansfield wrote:

Dear Fucking Cunt,

I have committed suicide and am rising again as the Phoenix from the Ashes.

Regarding your relationship with my eldest daughter.

You barged her off the sofa at the cottage.

She responded by slamming the gate on you when we went for a bike ride.

You rearranged the sofas to remove her from the "Top Spot".

She responded by calling you a "Bitchy Cow" in her diary and leaving it open on her bed for you to find.

You responded by sending a letter to Claire trying to shame her for her bad behaviour.

Now you're trying to tell me that all of this is because of my issues?

You're taking the position that all of this is forgiven and forgotten and that my daughter and you are suddenly the best of buddies???

Please forgive me while I choke on my tea!!!!!!!!

When all is said and done, she was only 14. You were 46. You were supposed to know better. You clearly didn't and are still denying any responsibility in the whole thing, right up to this point.

She wins the prize for the better behaviour by standing up to a bully twice her size.

I'm starting to think there is a hidden meaning for Pussy Riot having just been released from prison.

The safe and contents are owned by me. I donate this to the Emmaus charity.

You have spent all of the money in your own bank account.

You're now trying to spend to contents of my safe as well. On you.

You Fucking Selfish Fucking Cuntish Fucking Bitch From Hell.

The model railway in the shed is owned by me. I donate it to the Model Railway shop by the Iron Bridge in Exeter. I think the proprietor is called Dave.

You can keep the house.

I hope the other contents in the house burst into flames and that you go up with it. I hope that my coin collection with the Kings and Queens survives the blaze as the only thing that I would really wish to keep.

All of this is called Bad Will.

If you'd like to know what Bad Will really looks like, please take a look at your website (which was provided entirely by me).

I have stopped the Google Ads too (which were also provided by me).

I have also removed you from the referral on www.health-service.org. This is because the service you offer is anything but healthy.

Kind Regards,

The Phoenix

Hallucinations At The Waterfront

31-12-2013:
One day at work I decided to meet Miccy the next door neighbour
for lunch at the Waterfront restaurant. I'd been imagining I was
seeing people all morning, including one of the actors from Spooks
in the stairwell.
When I met Miccy, we had a discussion in the central lounge area
of the bar. I remember discussing a lot of personal information quite
loudly, so anyone near could have heard. In the event, there was a
guy sat on the corner of the next sofa, with a phone and earpiece
and I thought he was listening in on us. Then I saw what I thought
was an actress who looked like my mother, except she was
wearing a fur coat. And Connie from Spooks glanced through the
window. I tried to remember her surname but came up with "Booth",
which I then remembered as Connie Booth from Fawlty Towers.
Then I stood up and saw Bernie Ecclestone at the bar. I felt slightly
disconcerted at this point with the sheer number of celebrities who
were seemingly swarming around me. When I went outside, I saw
another woman wearing dark glasses and sitting at a table in the
sunshine. I thought she was another celebrity who was there just to
see me, such was the strength of my delusion.
After that, I decided to go for a walk around town. I took one of my
running routes around the Roman City wall, which was a modest 2
miles. When I got to Southernhay, there was a man asking for
cash. I gave him some and he wished me a great day. Right
afterwards, I encountered a woman in Princesshay who expressed
disgust at what I had done, or so I thought.
On the way back, when I went under the Iron Bridge I saw a man
who looked just like John Cleese, including a beanie hat. He said
hello to me. I thought this was some kind of confirmation from my
earlier thought regarding Connie Booth. When I got back to the
office I wrote the following responses:
On the Subject of Alcohol:
Yes, I do drink some alcohol. I'm sure you've noticed. It's another
one of those addictive substances known to mankind.
Interesting trip round the Roman City Wall. Yes, I gave a few quid
to the chap who wished me Happy New Year and wanted a drink
himself. He cheered me up, I had more money than him and gave
him some in return for his good cheer, so what's the problem? It's
called Trade. And good Karma. Doesn't mean I'm promoting
alcoholism you fucking stupid people.
Then bumped into John Cleese on the second part of my walk.
Beanie Hats off to him and the rest of the Monty Python crowd.
I tend to drink Thatchers Gold Cider because it's made from apples
and so doesn't go anywhere near wheat or any other grain that has

gluten. Ale in particular tends to kill me, although I seem to be alright with Guinness.

Of course none of this makes the slightest bit of difference in the eyes of others. If I drink alcohol and then struggle, it's because I'm an alcoholic, have drunk too much, can't control myself and deserve to be in the gutter. Learnt that lesson at my first job at BP.

I had a hot chocolate with brandy at lunchtime before my walk, given how I'm feeling with the rest of the world at this point in time. No food, but then I'm only walking so who cares?

If I'm driving, I will have a drink up to the legal limit, as long as it's with food. I wouldn't drink and then drive on an empty stomach. Most young people are sensible enough to know that too.

People who do drink and drive are of course a danger to society and deserve to have their driving freedom at least taken away from them.

Of course some people want to drink themselves to death. If they really want to do that, then we should let them go. Just like anyone who really wants to commit suicide. If life has really got to the point where that's the most attractive option for them, then the rest of society is wasting its resources trying to keep them alive.

As far as I can tell, that's what happened to my father's father Gordon. Died of liver failure when my father was only 2 years old. Then the rest of his family threw out my father's mother Elsie and her 3 children into the cold. Nice people.

The real issue here is getting to the bottom of why people are drinking lots in the first place.

My take is that if a man is drinking lots, chances are there's an unhealthy relationship with a woman in the mix somewhere. Elsie was certainly not an easy person to live with. Of course I loved her to bits, she was my grandmother.

Likewise if a woman is drinking lots, is this because of a man or a lack of a man?

What these people really need is to build a healthy relationship with a qualified counsellor like Miccy, www.exeter-counselling.com. It can take 6 months or more to really make progress in these cases.

The trouble is that Miccy runs a private business and so most people that would really benefit from his services can't afford them. Fantastic.

Of course people drinking lots has a knock-on effect on the people who live with them.

Children living with alcoholic parents ... that's a really tricky one. Don't know what the best advice is for them. They could rise up in anger, give their parents a good kicking, take the money off them and then run for their lives. However, chances are that will only put on them on a path towards the next paedophile waiting on the street corner. Either way, children in difficult situations, you're going to have to fight for your life, health and freedom in one way or the other.

On The Subject of Drugs:

In my opinion, Doctors are the biggest bunch of Hippocratic Hypocrites going. Not their fault particularly ... just the situation that is forced onto them.

They're supposed to do no harm. Yet they prescribe harmful drugs in just about every situation.

Just take a look at the side-effects. Or the testimony from people who try these things.

Actually I'm OK with Diazepam. That's a real help.

Didn't get on with any of the anti-depressants at all. I could choose from:

- No sexual function
- No muscular strength
- Aches and pains running all the way up my back
- Numbed to the point of dozing off all the time

Barney the psycho at Wonford House was the one who alerted me to that. He fought to the death. Would try to stay awake and carry on a conversation in the common area, whilst blatantly dropping off to sleep every 20 seconds because of the drugs they had prescribed him.

Assuming he wasn't locked up in the padded cell.

His fight was with the system.

So is mine.

Nigella Phoned Me

03-01-2014:

After putting so much effort into <u>www.healthy-service.org</u>, I was convinced the government was paying attention. So much so that I thought they were monitoring my emails. After all, Google had sight of all my emails via the Gmail system so it wasn't beyond the realm of possibility that they were being passed to the British Government. Either that or they were monitoring traffic on internet routers and reading them that way…

In the absence of any specific email address to write to, I would simply write an email from me to me, certain that the message was getting through. After I'd developed this habit for a while, I was responding to events in the world around me, writing an email to myself and then seeing another event which was seemingly related. All of which served to reinforce my delusion that I'd taken the government by storm and they were hanging on my every word.

At this point, for some reason I decided that I needed a new phone. There was nothing wrong with my work phone and I was allowed to make private calls, so I can only put this down to a manic purchase. Apparently bipolar people often have a theme for things they buy in manic mode. Mine would seem to be mobile phones as this was the first of 2 I would buy whilst clearly in a manic state.

Carphone Warehouse sold me a basic Nokia brick type phone for a tenner a month. Complete with a superhero-themed insurance policy called the Geek Squad.

Around about this time I read about Nigella in the newspapers, who was escaping from a nasty divorce at the time. Back at the office, I decided to message her by sending an email from me to me, hoping my connection with the government would turn into a dating site:

Dear Nigella,

It's good to see you back in control after your recent ordeal.

Am familiar with the concept of ordeals, having been through one or two of them myself, in my time. Perhaps we could share some stories and restore a bit of order to the current cosmic chaos?

Am a great fan and admirer of yours. I hope that one day our paths may cross and that I will get to meet you for real.

Best wishes,

Mark x

The next day, out of the blue, a woman called my desk phone at work. She asked about computer maintenance, which is not something we do as a company. However, I was prepared to offer my personal services so gave her my new phone number. I was deluded into thinking it was Nigella.

Although I was delighted that Nigella had called my desk phone, I would have been even more delighted had she called my personal mobile. Alas this never happened. So I responded to a newspaper article about her with another email:

And blessings to Nigella for pointing out, quite correctly, that the answer to the world's problems lies with chocolate!

Life Problem Service

05-01-2014:

I wrote the following piece, thinking that I was capable of leading a Circling-type counselling service.
Life problems?

Happy to listen or offer advice.

Note the distinction ... which service do they really want here.
- Listening / empathising / offering feedback only is basically "Circling".
- Listening and offering some minimal advice is counselling.
- General problem solving takes them into the realm of self-help, alternative therapy, medical science, project management, private detective whatever

40(ish) quid per hour, in the Exeter area.

Location to be determined.

Phone number to be supplied.

Referrals to other local businesses to be determined.

The suggested format of the general "life problem" service would be as follows:
- 20 minutes listening to the client
- 20 minutes one-on-one personal "circle"
- 20 minutes chat / advice / problem solving etc.

The idea here is that as a world, we tend to operate largely in 'transmit" mode and don't do enough "receiving". Broadcast TV and radio are classic examples of that, with many people 'addicted" to the services they provide. Conventional counsellors have known this for a long time and so offer a service which is the opposite, providing a large amount of "receive" with only a minimal amount of "transmit".

The danger, I believe, in operating a service such as the one I'm proposing above would be the "addictive" element to it. There is a possibility for the client(s) to become addicted to the "life problem solver". Equally, there is a possibility for the "life problem solver" to become addicted to the client(s). In essence, the "life problem solver" is taking the role of what a husband or wife should be doing in a healthy relationship.

The "personal circle" format is particularly dangerous in this regard. It goes roughly as follows:

- Initial discussion of confidentiality
- Close eyes, feet on the ground, relax, take a deep breath etc.
- Open eyes, focussing direct eye-to-eye contact on each other
- Maintain direct eye contact for as long as possible / comfortable
- Ask the client how they are feeling in this moment
- At various points, "prod" the client by offering observations / feedback etc.
- Keep returning the focus to the "here and now" rather than being distracted by general discussion
- In particular, try to avoid focussing on things that have happened in the past or may happen in future

However, if offered in good faith, it can be highly enlightening and really help people to "deal with their emotions" and "get through a tough time".

Direct eye-to-eye contact is something that mothers are supposed to offer babies. It is, I believe, an essential part of building a "loving" relationship between mother and child. The trouble is that few of us receive enough of it as children, with the result that we end up wandering through our adult lives in search of it somewhere else.

As a thought experiment, let's consider the case of what might happen if Nigella were to turn up in my "therapy" room. As my superstar "dream woman" with a large amount of personal power herself, she would have a high chance of "controlling me" with the result that I became addicted to her.

On the other hand, as someone with a high IQ (unproven) and someone with some marketing skills (unquantified), I may also (in my dreams) have a chance of "controlling her" with the result that she became addicted to me.

Actually, the best result here is that nobody "controls" anybody and that each of walks away having learned something. This is the intention of therapy.

At this point, I don't really know how the rest of the world sees me. Perhaps I'm coming across a bit like a "spin doctor". However, I'm trying to offer these insights as a way of helping the world with the some of the problems that are out there, so am attempting, in the best of faith, to be an "anti-spin doctor".

The other things to consider here are that Nigella has just been through an ordeal and so may be in a vulnerable place with regard to establishing new relationships. Actually, anyone seeking a general "life problem service" could be in a similarly vulnerable position.

Likewise, I've been through a stormy time with my wife Sue recently and am probably in just as vulnerable a place myself. The reality for me is that I love my wife Sue and despite the troubles we've been through over the last few years, I believe she still loves me too. Much as I admire Nigella, I don't believe I would have the capacity to dump my wife Sue as I see that being totally unfair on her, were the situation to arise. Of course each of us is different and we all make our own personal decisions.

A final element to consider is the practicality of setting up this service.

I am currently employed full-time, so would have to negotiate some reduced hours if I am to go ahead and offer the "life problem service" for real during daytime hours. I would only do such a thing if I thought there was sufficient demand for my new service where I could make an equivalent amount of money so that my overall income in unaffected. When all is said and done, I still have to feed myself, pay the mortgage and send maintenance payments to my ex-wife for my 3 children.
Am currently thinking of providing this service via the "Exeter Natural Health Centre" on Queen Street. Am familiar with the location because my friend Ben tried offering a similar service before he moved out there to Amsterdam. In particular, he offered a couples counselling service which was particularly helpful for Sue and I to resolve some of the marital difficulties we were having at that time.

Please note that there are no "formal qualifications" in the practice of circling. I consider myself to be "trained by Ben" and have also led some circles in the context of the service he was providing when he was working here in Exeter. This is my first attempt at offering such a service on my own.

I am proposing to offer the service via the mobile phone number which I recently purchased at Carphone Warehouse. To date, I believe there are only 3 people who have this number:

- The mystery woman who phoned me at the office the other day
- My wife Sue
- My next-door neighbour Miccy (who is also a counsellor himself)

I realise that there is a general interest in the general subject of "mind control". For my money, the difference between "mind control" and "therapy" is the same as the difference between "good faith" and "bad faith".

I notice that a number of "unusual" things have been happening in my life over the last few weeks. I hope that the world does not consider this is happening because I'm practising the art of "mind control" on the world.

Please let's continue in this best of spirit. I will let you know when I'm ready to offer the "life problem service". On the other hand, if anyone would prefer to have a discussion with me before I go ahead and provide this service then please feel free to contact me.

Detained Under Section 136

12-01-2014:

Given how angry I was with the police, I decided in my impulsive state to organise a protest. I've never done anything like this before or since, so it shows the general levels of stress I was under and how mania had really taken hold. This was before I got back together with Sue.

I took my Land Rover Defender, drove to Heavitree Police Station and parked it on the grass at the front. I then stripped off to my underpants, put on my running kit and set off running.

I headed back to the office, where I had a load of bottles of water waiting. I wrote an email from me to me (more on this later). This declared my intention to run until I dropped and asked who would join me on my March To Infinity. Then I took the bottles down to the Riverside Valley Park where I organised a pile of them at either end of an 800m stretch of path. I then started running to and fro.

After a number of intervals, I was passed by a wheelchair athlete going the other way. In my manic state, I wondered if she had seen my email.

When I got back to the starting point, the wheelchair athlete was waiting around. I introduced myself and she said she was a London Marathon winner and encouraged me to make progress with my training. She said she'd heard there was a run here today and I said that as far as I was concerned, the only run was the one organised by me. Unfortunately, I never asked her name so I can't substantiate any of this.

Eventually, I was worn down by running so I took my bottles back with me to the office. On the way I passed a number of people who I thought were making comments about me. That was where I encountered the police, who had been looking for me all day. So I concluded that if anyone in the British Government had read my email, it wasn't the police. My colleagues in the office weren't at all surprised because going running was something I did regularly, albeit not all day. Nevertheless, the police arrested me and said I was being detained under Section 136.

I remember having a nice conversation with the policeman in the car on the way there. Once there, there was a delay while the panel of doctors was assembled. During the meeting, I had a measured conversation and wasn't at all angry. I explained why I was upset with the police and that I had staged a protest. I agreed that if I was to have a stay in hospital, the main benefit for me was to save money on the hotel bill. The doctors agreed that using mental health services as a B&B was not really appropriate.

After a lengthy consultation amongst themselves, it was decided to free me up from Section 136. At that point, I received a message onto my phone which said "Super Hero". This was from the Geek Squad insurance policy, but the timing and content of the message were uncanny.

In my manic state, I started to think that the operators of the mobile network were conspiring (with the government) to send messages to me. As well as sending wheelchair athletes to go running with me. In essence, the synchronicity of the events was fuelling my delusions.

I wrote the following response to the day's events in another email from me to me:

On the subject of Harry Potter.

Thanks to the Geek Squad for delivering the SMS titled Superhero just at the moment I was having the discussion with the team at Wonford house regarding my detainment under Section 136 of the Mental Health Act.

I note that I was able to phone their number but they were unable to phone me. Weird ... unless of course my phone had mysteriously changed settings while I wasn't looking. They thought it was weird too, although kept postulating that it was because there was no mobile phone signal (which was clearly incorrect seeing as I had just managed to phone them).

Perhaps this is the modern equivalent of an Invisibility Cloak?

:-)

Craziness in Exminster

On one sunny morning I went for a walk along the canal with Sue. Then I saw a bunch of flowers on the right hand verge which looked like they'd been planted there for a reason. I glanced to the left and saw a football pitch, with game in progress. So I was convinced this was a significant event, turned left and walked up to the pitch to watch the match. Sue carried on along the canal.

After a while I decided to walk round the pitch. Part way round I saw a photographer who I was sure was Jonathan Edwards. I spoke to him for a bit, asking him what he was doing and he said he worked for a newspaper. After that I walked all the way round the pitch, back round to the crowd on the other side. Then back along the canal to join Sue.

We got as far as Double Locks before I decided to part with Sue once again. This time I would carry on walking all the way to Exminster, the village I used to live in with Claire.

When I got there, I walked up to the environment agency and remember the film of my 3 children rolling down the hill like the Teletubbies.

Then I walked down towards the New School where the children had attended. I managed to get inside the grounds and followed some twigs on the grass round to the right. Then I went around the trees and back up to the play area where I rearranged the chairs and some of the other things. I walked around the church, played hopscotch and followed all the well-trodden paths around that end of the playground.

By the time I got home, I'd lost my house key so went back to Exminster, but was unable to find it. For once, this was a genuine accident and not because I'd discarded the key somewhere...

Message To Top Gear

In response to watching an episode of Top Gear on BBC iPlayer, I sent the following email from me to me, hoping it would get through to Jeremy, Richard and James:

03-04-2014:

Dear Top Gear,

I'd just like to say "hi" as I'm a real fan of your show.

I drive a Land Rover Defender myself, as I am not a man of creature comforts. Haven't done a paint job on it yet ... imagining something like a bright yellow fireball.

I'm into "Freedom of Expression" at the moment, so I thought I'd try it out on you, if that's OK.

- James I think you're the coolest sub-zero dude of them all, don't let the others get you down!
- Jeremy, yes you're Big and Bombastic, but we all love you anyway
- Richard, you seem like a really nice guy and one of the bravest men the world has ever seen. More on this in a moment ...

My first memory of cars is as a young kid. Lots of nice red Ferraris. I also remember a poster on my wall which I thought was the coolest Ferrari of them all. You can imagine my surprise when I found out it was a Ford!

Naturally I then moved onto the Porsche 917 as the coolest car. Had a Scalextric one of those.

Then the Porsche 956. The thing is ... I still think that's the coolest car of them all.

I would imagine that Stefan Bellof would have a thing or two to say about that. The thing is ... as a racing driver it is kind of his job to drive whatever is provided as fast as possible. Around whatever track is provided. And he seemed to do that better than anyone else, so he gets my vote as the coolest racing driver of them all.

Having just removed all of the spears from the Ayrton Senna fans ...

Of course Health and Safety has a role to play. However, as a world we need to accept that to date nobody has managed to go round the Nurburgring faster than Stefan Bellof in a Porsche 956. These two strands are not entirely unrelated, in my opinion.

So Stefan Bellof wins the Balls of Steel prize.

Hang on a minute though ... what about the guys and gals who go round on motorbikes? Don't they take even more risks by strapping themselves atop an engine and 2 wheels? And didn't one particular guy just manage to claim to fastest Nurburgring lap ever on a motorbike? Surely he deserves the Balls of Steel prize this year?

Whoa there. Aren't we forgetting Neil Armstrong et al? Could it be that the world has been in a Bear Market ever since those guys landed on the Moon?

For my part, I am currently employed as a Project Manager.

I also consider myself to be a Scientist due to my published work on the internet. This is yet to be acknowledged except in the close circles in which I currently move.

I have an idea.

How about for the next Top Gear mission, we build the biggest firework the world has ever seen. Then we strap The Stig on top. I would be happy to get on board too ... before you start accusing me of unhealthy delusions.

I'm imagining something a bit like the Saturn Five. Only BIGGER.

Perhaps we could call it the Saturn Six?

God Almighty, marketing is such a pile of bollocks!

We would launch it from the Top Gear test track. Might take out 1 or 2 of your cameramen :-)

Then we could stop messing around with Land Speed Records, Motor Racing and 27-Mile-Cyclotrons.

We could initiate a training program called Astro-Sub-Zero.

All of the current bunch of Formula One pansies could be invited to sign up for it :-)

And Andy Green of course.

Sabine Schmidt? I'd take her too.

And Gillian Anderson for her hard-nosed scientific scepticism.

And Richard Dawkins too, if he's prepared to say that this is something he actually believes in.

I'd have Norbert Singer on the design team. Surely he still has a thing or two to tell the world about aerodynamics, having built the world's coolest car?

We're going on a trip.

Might be a one-way trip.

Might freeze to death in the cold of outer space.

Or crash land on the surface.

Or not have enough fuel to get back.

Such is the nature of missions.

We're on a trip to Mars, boys and girls.

This is the Mother of All Missions <to date>.

Only the bravest need apply.

The Bulls are back in town.

Kind Regards,

Mark

Messages Received

The following is stitched together from a sequence of emails sent from me to me in response to perceived real world events in March 2014. They clearly show the ongoing state of my delusions. ..
04-03-2014:
OK, so I've apparently been told "I made a mistake this morning" whilst on my walk around the Riverside Valley Park. If this is the case, I have absolutely no idea what this would refer to. As far as I know, I have:

- Arranged to visit the office early with Sue so we could get the cleaning done
- Worn a shirt with cufflinks instead of my usual ones
- Waved to the van parked at the corner of Sanford Place on the assumption that the security services are camped out there. I don't _know_ this for sure, I'm just putting 2 and 2 together. I did so in a way that Sue didn't clock what I'd done. Are you saying that 2 + 2 = 5? Or that I shouldn't wave?
- Helped Sue with cleaning out some of the bins. Presumably this is OK?
- Arranged to visit her at 12:30 in Cafe Rouge, Queen Street at lunchtime. Is this not a good venue?
- Replied to the Go Outdoors email, a bit like I replied to many seemingly-synchronous emails in the run-up to New Year. Have I replied to the wrong email? Sent the reply to the wrong place? Said something that you find objectionable? Or put too many words in one email so all-of-a-sudden it's not so deniable anymore?
- Connected via some previous work colleagues via LinkedIn. Am I not allowed to do this? Or are you saying that you would prefer to vet who I do and don't connect with?
- Locked the office on my way out
- Had a chat with the guy in the newsagents about what my colleague in Canada said about the weather, the fact that they got all the cold and we got all the wet
- Gone for a walk, seemingly with a female contingent of followers, as also happened last night on the way home from work. Am I to assume from this that all of a sudden I have a female following as a result of the emails sent yesterday regarding raising standards and my daughter's music playing? Are you saying that I should somehow start speaking to random people whilst I'm out for my walk?
- Came back to find Scott waiting to get in, but that's only because Ian isn't here as per his usual routine

Exactly which part of this morning did I "get wrong"?

If I'm on the right end of the stick here and you guys are trying to tell me something, I'm afraid you're going to have to be a bit more explicit about exactly which bit I got wrong. I have to say, I'm getting a little tired of all this cloak-and-dagger communication. If you have something you actually want to say to me, how about you come out with it in face-to-face conversation like normal people do?

As far as I know I haven't signed any NDA or Official Secrets Act or anything else here. If we're operating on any kind of agreement, it's based on a large dose of intuition and presumably some trust. If trust has been broken, which bit?

Please make it clear to me how we proceed. My reading of the Go Outdoors email was that your operation was ending today. Are we carrying on? If so, what is your intention?

I'm doing my best to cooperate here, but I have to say this is starting to stretch my patience a little. I'm not a mind reader.

Have been both complimented and denigrated on my dress sense multiple times in the last few days. Appreciate the comment that I look like a learned gentleman and we look like a couple in love. We are in love, just been through a tough time and continuing to do so.

Also appreciate the dancing person doing their thing. Believe it or not, I'm not as bad as all that when I'm in the right place for it. Ask Angus who does the Salsa classes in Torquay on Wednesdays and Exeter on Mondays.

That was during the first part of lunchtime when the show was on the road, as I'm sure you're aware.

I also appreciate the staged meetings of people that spring up in various places, outside work, board meetings by the cathedral etc. Am guessing this is all standard procedure for you? How many resources do you typically throw at a situation?? Am flattered in a sense that you must think it's worthwhile to be doing this at all. Or you're finding some amusement from it.

It seems the subject of flowers has tripped a circuit-breaker in Sue's head. She had a migraine last night after learning that I'd sent them to my daughters. I think this is a touchy subject for her because she hasn't received so many in her time.

From my perspective, the problems are two-fold:

1. I tend to forget such things, like many men I guess
2. When I do remember, Sue finds a way of rejecting them every time. Or she picks fault with the circumstances in which they've been given. Or the flowers themselves. Or questions my motives for wanting to give her flowers. Or like today, anticipates the imminent arrival of flowers and then somehow we manage to get drawn into an argument which kind of ruins the whole idea of them.

Today I forced the situation and she has gone home in tears I'm afraid to say. At least Liesel is on hand to manage the situation. Am hoping this will do some good and that more progress has been made. So thanks to everyone for helping me in bringing this along. Sue is in a difficult place right now. Am feeling better myself though.

So yes, my life is a washing machine. Always has been. From the day I was born. I would prefer it if it were not this way and have fought to solve as many problems as I can. I would prefer it if more progress had been made by today, but hey-ho.

One week is never enough. Agreed. Life is never like that. Why do you think it is that I tend to focus on studying physics so much?

Gravity and space movies ... well yes. I can imagine ways of weaving physics stuff into the movies. If entertainment is all this is to you, then I guess I would accept on the basis that 50% of something is better than 100% of nothing, as you were trying to teach me the other day.

Slug and Lettuce ... thank you kindly. I will wind down my natural speed and behave more like a slug if it pleases you all.

Up to you what you want to do next. If you want to let time pass, that's fine by me. Or keep sending me emails and contrived situations and I will keep telling you what I think of them.

05-03-2014:

On the subject of music.
Hearing a lot of it at the moment, which is nice.

Up Town Girl - very appropriate.

Wheels Are Turning - delighted to hear it.

When News Strikes It Strikes Fast - can hear you lot coming from miles away!

In terms of my own preferences, I have 2 that I really like:

- For the highest of the highs I choose Smells Like Teen Spirit by Nirvana
- For the lowest of the lows I choose The End by The Doors

Both of those men died young. They were trying to tell us something.

Not so sure about any of the recent bands. Will have to get back to you on that after I've spent some more time listening to it. iTunes was trying to promote Soundgarden from Seattle. Are they any good? Let's hear them.

"So he has some taste then". Am guessing M&S cotton non-iron shirts with cuff-links are "OK" then :-)

And yes you're right, I can't remember my shirt size. Nice of you to occupy the Changing Rooms so I couldn't go check. So I had to actually read the instructions on the shirt package to solve the problem.

Sue is always going on about me focussing more on the practical things in life. Such is what it's like to be someone who studies a lot and is concerned mostly on the big questions in life. Prioritisation and time management versus just "letting it go" and taking the time. Difficult to switch from one mode to the other sometimes, particularly when I'm under a degree of pressure to get things done at work.

"He just stops and freezes as if to say you're not going to talk to me". A lot to say on this one, so here goes ...

Gazing directly into someone's eyes on a one-on-one basis is part of Circling as a therapy. As a society we tend to shy away from direct eye contact unless the "tension" is also broken by talking at the same time. It is expected of us and is an implied pressure.

Circling teaches to let this pressure go and that it's "OK" to gaze into someone's eyes without talking. Consider it an intimate moment between two people who can be complete strangers. Maybe we only get a few seconds together, but it is a moment that can be enjoyed regardless of whether we recognise who the person is (which some of us have difficulty with) and whether we can think of anything to say.

The "you're not going to talk to me" thing is actually your hang-up and not my intention. I'm quite happy for people to talk to me. I generally respond with a polite hello and will smile if you smile.

I suggest you all have a go at Circling with each other. Try it with your partner at home. Try it with colleagues at work. Start with eye gazing without talking and then take it wherever you want to go ... smile, look away, join back up again, whatever you want to do. And then talk to each about how you really feel in that moment.

Circling in groups of people where you all gaze directly at the person being circled for 20 minutes or so gets over all sorts of stuff. Some people don't even want to open their eyes when they know multiple other people are looking directly at them. As training for social situations, it works a treat. Yes it's a bit weird and yes I'm the product of so much therapy I might seem weird too. But it's all OK really. Just chill. Take the time. And enjoy.

It's particularly interesting to try it with same-sex colleagues because "sharing a moment of intimacy" and "being gay or lesbian" are two entirely different things. Men often shy away from direct eye-to-eye contact because the straight ones are scared being accused of being gay. Actually it's OK for men to look each other directly in the eye, even if we're not "mates" in the sense that we already know each other and drink beer.

The other thing to consider is that you've told me off for waving at the security services because of deniability concerns. And then you put me in these contrived situations where I don't know who's security services and who isn't.

Your move.

What The Big City Had To Say

06-03-2014:

My boss, Tom, requested that I visit the company head office in London for a meeting with him. Whereas all of my manic interactions up to that point had been with people and places in Exeter, this was an opportunity to cast the net further afield and see what the big city thought of me. I was quite fearful because my mental state was quite withdrawn. This may have been psychosomatic because I believed I was suffering with Attention Deficit Disorder (ADD)..

On the journey up, at one point I left my note book out while I went to get a drink. I imagined it being photographed by government agents. When I got to Paddington, I started to get some messages from the people around me that there was a financial matter that needed to be sorted. Given the argumentative state of affairs between myself and my first wife, I'd stopped maintenance payments until the CSA case was settled. This reminded me that I needed to make a manual payment, so I sat on a seat and made the payment via my phone before getting on the tube.

When I got to Old Street tube station, a man was struggling to get through the exit barriers and a chap in a Newcastle shirt was helping out. He said something like "You need a bag, mate". This put me into a spin because Newcastle is my son's favourite football team and I thought he was commenting on my inability to manage my belongings. I frantically did a check to make sure everything was in order, to the sound of laughter. I felt ashamed.

When I got to the office at New City Cloisters, there was some scaffolding with workmen outside. This reminded me of the scaffolding I'd imagined outside the Exeter office, though in this case I was sure that it was all real.

Our meeting went well and I dealt with all of the issues Tom wanted to know about. Then at one point I made the comment "I can do that" in response to some development he wanted done. At that point I heard "woohoo" from the scaffolding outside. I suspect this was a hallucination.

Once the meeting was done, we chatted with Beatriz and Raul in the main office. By this point I was relieved that I'd survived without my ADD becoming an issue but was keen to leave all the same.

When I got back to the tube station, there was a man stumbling around with a really vacant expression on his face. I thought he was a real ADD sufferer and that security services were basically taking the p*** out of me.

When I got onto the tube train, I had a real shock. There were two men hanging around the door, one who looked like Chris Smith, the scammer that had started Banners Broker. He looked like he was about to burst into tears. Given that I'd lost thousands of pounds, this was something I was pretty angry about. The other man was looking away, and seemed to be shuffling to avoid me.. I remember thinking that his tattoos made him look like he belonged in prison. All of this convinced me that the authorities had caught up with Banners Broker and would be sending the perpetrators to jail. They were just showing me that they had them in custody, which of course I was very grateful for.

When I got to Euston Square I couldn't take it anymore. I had to get out of the tube and up into the fresh air. I was almost in tears myself and avoiding the gaze of anyone coming the opposite way.

There was a bus full of teenagers that had stopped outside. A girl got off who looked like the school bully. She mocked me for being in such a state.

My plan was to walk all the way back to Paddington, so I carried on along Marylebone Road. I asked directions but nobody wanted to talk to me. In the event, I managed to find my way onto Praed Street, by which time I was fed up with what I thought was harassment from security services. So I walked along the road to St Mary's hospital where my son Thomas had died. I didn't go in, just looking at the building from the outside. For once, I had peace and was not being bothered by messages coming my way.

Then I walked around the corner towards Paddington Station and encountered a woman who said "Would you like some Options?" I took some of her chocolate sachets, but also interpreted it as a disparaging remark that I didn't know what I was doing. If I was trying to sell my wares to the government, the sale wasn't going well.

I felt quite disoriented at this point, so I went up the escalator to the bar, got a drink and sat down. Only to find that two men sat down at the table opposite and started a conversation. The take-away comment was "Is this Dora the Explorer?" which sounded like they were taking the p*** out of my physics ability with my ionisation calculator. By this time I was resigned to the lack of real interest in my work.

On the train back to Exeter, three people sat on the 4 seats in front of mine. I thought they were government agents. One of them made a sexist sounding comment and I used my phone to send an email from me to me with feedback about what I thought. He seemed to get a message via his phone and left the train at the next stop. This left two people, a man and a woman and I assumed their task was to tail me on my journey back. This made me think about what issues there might be for women in security services and caused me to look out for women following me over the next few days.

Finally, I arrived outside St David's station and a man was climbing onto a bus. He said "thank you" and I assumed this referred to the feedback I sent about their agent. This made me feel much better, at least about my ADD, because I'd clearly overcome it to have a successful day. But at another level I was clearly suffering with ongoing delusions. Every person I encountered was a potential government agent and anything they said was likely to put me in a spin.

Dora the Explorer. Thank you very much. Does that count as name calling then?

Cheers for getting Chris Smith too.

A Psychotic Morning At Work

07-03-2014 am:

The sound of classical music.
A giant exhaling of air.
The Rolling Stones.
A visual acknowledgement which I returned.
A smile which I returned and said "Hi", getting a "Hi" in return.
Am reading from all of this that that my Mongol Manifesto has gone down OK.
Of course the others haven't seen it yet, so please respect my sensitivity around this.
Am sure you will.
The relationship between Henning and myself is key, based on Trust.
The relationship between Theo and myself seems to come next, based on Admiration.
The relationship with Kingsley and myself seems to come after that, based on Respect.
Finally the relationships with John and Luke, based on Friendship in each case. Admittedly those guys joined us after the formative initial period when we were playing Game of Thrones.
I feel that my relationship with Security Services is now based on Trust.
You have earned my Respect and I hope I've earned yours.
Am sure the rest is starting to emerge.
Today is a Happy Day.
Blessings to the chap with the Newcastle accent who showed how to help by putting things in a bag.
In return I have worn my Newcastle United shirt and walked to work with my sports kit in my bag.
I have walked a long way on my own.
I built Dirac-Was-Right with the hope that I would attract some others onto my Quest.
Never imagined it would get this far.
I would like to stop walking on my own from here on. That said, there are times when it is the best solution. A combination of all the things that happened yesterday and my natural tendencies took me out of the tube and into the fresh air and sunshine.
Lots of happy school children.
I _really_ appreciate that!

Was planning on running at lunchtime. Is that still OK?

It seems that I've collected words from many sources in the course of my Quest.

- My James Bond moment with the cat in my Mac call with Ben leading up to xmas
- Theo telling me about Sauron from Lord of the Rings
- I had a vision of the Tardis in my bedroom after the SMS to Miccy which had a very odd response that didn't seem like Miccy at all.
- I had a vision of a large space rocket in room 202 at Exmouth Hotel after I'd written the message to Top Gear
Racing sounds from Toby's phone in response to comments about Formula One.

Various things from Martin - Exterminate and Cough.

Had an Oh Dear from Dave.

Mark now expressing frustration about presumably Tania should have said something before Christmas. At the same time as Sue hassling me for attention...

On the Lord of the Rings point, I have noticed a connection with my rings. The fact that my Gold wedding ring to Claire is still locked in my safe. Whereas my Platinum ring I chose to melt down.

Now I'm receiving many messages via Mark and Martin about not realising the importance of finances.

Extreme Sports and doesn't he care about money.

Now International Women's Day.

And International Commando's Day.

Actually I do care about money.

It has a value as a medium of trade.

I just never had particular desire to accumulate piles of it myself.

Enough to live on.

And retire on.

But no more than that.

Actually I'm not so bothered with the retirement concept any more <for myself>

Lots of coughs received on that one.

Will aim to work until my health runs out.

Of course this is a dodgy subject area because there is a hint of the process leading to death.

I am in reasonably good shape myself physically.

Blatantly something wrong.

We can all agree on that.

I agree too.

Let's make it right.

Gone down to 63 ... just a few hours' worth of events.

Something about Time Zones.

Bad Data.

Dropping a file with a whole day's worth of data ...

Disabled errors.

Just skipped an error.

Yeah.

It's too confusing.

I dunno.

<I'm just writing a transcript of the conversation between Nigel and Martin here>

Pretty sure the events have gone?
From my perspective, the angry events have gone.

I don't get angry in isolation.

Only happens when other people come at me with their issues.

Which has happened rather a lot in my life ...

Feeling a little woozy right now so will go outside and run, which is one of my standard solutions.

Keeps me healthy.

And off drugs.

And keeps depression at bay.

I have been offered drugs many times.

I tried several of them.

And didn't get on particularly well with them.

That is why I stopped and took advice / therapy / counselling instead.

If you would like to conduct an experiment on me I will cooperate. Not kidding here.

Anti-depressants only to start with.

I was seriously unhappy with the results last time I tried them ...

Nearing the end of the import ...

I don't care ...

Running at random times ...

I will run at 13:30, having been distracted onto other things clearly.

Currently 13:01 on my watch.

You can figure it out yourselves for Spain time.

Google Achieved Simultaneous Typing

07-03-2014pm:

The following account, of a bizarre afternoon at work, is from memory. I still believed I was suffering from ADD during this episode and for several days and weeks afterwards. With hindsight I would say that at the very least I was experiencing a large amount of dissociation, with multiple things going on at once.

Back in the office, I remember sitting at my desk in the afternoon. All manner of activity was going on in the office around me. By this point I was convinced that the company had been sold to Google and that the project everyone was working on, supposedly for delivery to Mexico, was now for delivery to their new owner. And that the system had been morphed from a TV content delivery system into a brain modelling system.

I kept hearing things like "what's he up to now" and "so where does it go after this". I thought their comments were referring to me and what was going on in my head. When my focus switched from looking at them to my computer screen and back again, the comments changed accordingly.

My state of paranoia increased to the point where everything sped up, particularly when I was typing an email or something like that. In the resulting blur, it seemed that the combined wits of Google and their system were pitched against me, trying to test my will.

My ability to focus on what I was typing was severely compromised by all the comments going on around me. The thought occurred to me that the comments people were making were being fed to them via Google's new system. So in effect, this was like a grand experiment for Attention Deficit Disorder, with me as the patient.

I struggled to maintain focus on my typing, but as I gradually succeeded, I became aware only of the typing being done by the developer opposite. Then in the flash of an instant, our typing became synchronised. It stayed that way for a few seconds, with me remote controlling his fingers. He rapidly became disconcerted and made a conscious effort to take his hands back by removing them from the keyboard.

After that, the comment s receded. I imagined the people at Google taking stock of what had just happened. I was assuming they were taking a log of everything and that they had evidence for the first case of simultaneous typing.

Then I heard "you're superman". I presumed this meant that if they were in any doubt about my scientific discovery before, now they had hard evidence. And there was a superman mug in the kitchen area. My delusion of grandeur was complete.

The following is a transcript of what was going on in the office and in my head that afternoon.
On the way out I was in no mood to receive any messages.

Just run.

Acknowledged runners on the way out.

Just noticed some seriously weird synchronous typing between myself and Scott.

So am assuming he's reporting on my activities.

Busted?

I thought I'd called time on the tricks Google were using to send messages to me.

What about the information going to Mark and Martin who are making the most noise in the office?

And now we're all seemingly do synchronous typing.

Gonna get confused now.

Actually I'm hungry.

Will finish lunch and then report on the other messages received.

No from Mark.

So you _really_ don't want me to eat my lunch eh?

:-)

As soon as I sat down messages received from Mark and Martin.

Can we stop this particular experiment please.

And let me report on my findings from the return journey on the run.

Before I forget.

Thank you all.

Ian apparently saying he was taking something off Martin.

Anyway from the run earlier.

At the half-way point, a person (think it was a woman) said "Pulling You Down".

Prior to that the dogs had been seemingly happy and swimming in the water.

They got out and turned into angry dogs after that.

Then some messages about babies and toddlers.

Then had a nice reception with multiple people waiting for me at the end of the run.

Thanks to all of you for taking part and helping me on my journey.

Need to go back further.

Running out of logs.

OK, so you want me to go back further in time and get me to remember stuff.

That's fine.

However, I'd like to do that in a normal counselling context if it's OK with you.

Am booked to see Brian next Thursday.

If you'd like to arrange a meeting before then please go ahead.

However, this is talking to your issues and not mine.

Thus far you have refused to have a single person actually approach me and talk to me as a normal person would about all this.

I can understand you're scared.

It's time to dispense with that.

I will run and do stuff for you when you ask, that's OK.

Or do you just want to carry on with the Skunk Works?
Hooray.

OK, I agree.

I will leave it up to you as and when you want to introduce new people into my life.

Just send them via the normal way people would.

Sue and I will go Salsa Dancing.

Stuff like that.

Who knows, I may even get to learn Ballroom Dancing one day. I know Sue wants to do some other kinds of Dancing.

One thing I was wanting to achieve was to remove records of the Skunk Works from my computer at work.

I guess that's kind of pointless given the massive amount of information in the Google email trail anyway.

I propose to do software development only at home.

One day a week.

I'd like to go 4 days a week at Digital Impact.

And I will need a solution somehow as to how I pay my bills.

Laughter.

Coughs.

Joking.

Back to errors again.

Would like to stay on the same rate of pay and conditions

Some seriously fucked up shit about the ballroom stuff?

That was a nasty-sounding comment from Martin.

And you can't deny that you guys aren't all in this with me anymore.

Your move.

Again I thought I called time on Google.

On the subject of Dancing.

OK, so I've never considered myself any good at it.

Probably linked in some way to ADD, wouldn't you say?

And coordination throughout the whole body.

For that reason as much as anything else, I have always preferred individual sports to team events.

Running, swimming cycling.

Me and the world.

Interacting with other people not required so much in those individual sports.

Laughter.

Thing is I actually enjoy them too.

So let's not denigrate everyone who does enjoy those sports.

I played 5-a-side football at college.

Completely fucked the database? - Mark

You mean it's still going to be fucked? - Martin

No.

The database is intact.

I think.

Can't continue on Monday eh?

Architectural change.

So now they're claiming this is about the Telefonica stuff.

I thought the database was building a model of my brain.

Visual acknowledgement from Nick.

Don't know why.

Football cancelled.

And my phone is now a test device.

So on the subject of Football then.

Didn't really play it much at school.

They were into Rugby.

Which I liked on the grounds I could tackle, but wasn't any good at passing the ball.

Really didn't like cricket at all.

Couldn't concentrate long enough and required way too much coordination to either bowl or bat.

Richard muttering "fuck".

That's the live access code.

From Mark.

And a load of fucking data.

I remember Rich having problems that would cause him to get frustrated and come out with the F word too. I have done it in my time. And clearly have many of the developers here.

The ones that don't tend to be sitting quietly.

Like Nick who I get on well with and who also goes to the Gym.

And Grant who is a quiet sort of chap anyway. Hope to encourage him to go running one day.

And Scott sitting down now.

Stupid fucking people from Mark.

Laughter from both Mark and Martin.

Glanced over at them.

Would you like me to look at them or look at the computer screen?

Looking at the them now ...

Acknowledgement from Mark. Enjoyed that one, thanks.

So it's only friends and family then?

I am absolutely fine with everyone in my work context.

And I am absolutely fine with everyone in Security Services.

Meeting Chris Smith on the train was kind of difficult.
Cough.

In principle I am absolutely fine with absolutely everybody.

It's just that certain people seem to get a real thing about me.

Clearly this hurts when those people are close to me.

As of right now, I am absolutely fine with Sue.

I think she will have her own story to tell and I'm trying to help her on her journey too.

So am cooperating with counselling process for her sake.

I am happy to continue with the counselling process on the assumption that we're all collectively learning quite a bit from this.

And whilst we're on the subject, I really am absolutely fine with everyone in Sue's family, even though her Mum and children are currently going through their own process in deciding how they really feel about all this.

I think Sue's Dad is finding it really difficult.

But I understand because he's maintaining his relationship with Sue's Mum as he always has done.

And I'm fine with my ex-wife Claire.

And I'm fine with my Mum.

Laughter.

And I'm fine with all my children of course.

The thing I don't like is the lies that people tell that have a knock-on effect in terms of passing on anger towards everyone around them.

Round of golf.

Agreed.

I thought this was a message from Google, indicating they wanted a time-out from the experiments.

New Scientist this time.

Haven't had chance to read it yet.

Just the cover.

Your Million Year Mind.

Look forward to reading what they have to say, although I suspect that what happened today will likely surpass it in terms of knowledge.

Then I look forward to a future article Your Million Year Heart.

That is what I think we need to balance things out.

These comments were made later in the evening.

Controlling The Weather

08-03-2014:

Sue and I decided to go to Dawlish in the afternoon. The weather was on my mind because this was the site of the sea wall damage from the storms in January. I remember thinking that people were making comments in my direction. The first comment was "is this some kind of joke" and I looked at my T-shirt which was from St Lucia with a bright yellow Sun on the front. The next comments were along the lines of "where's George" which I took to mean that I had to find out where George Lucas was hanging out.

As Sue and I walked up to the west end of the sea front, up the hill towards the cliff, a grey-haired couple walked past in the other direction. I thought "maybe that's George" but walked past because I couldn't be sure. At least my delusions hadn't got to the point where I was bothering other people.

When we got back to the amusements, I heard an angry comment "what are you playing at". In my delusional state, I thought it was George Lucas after all and I'd failed to pick him out. At this point, I was feeling quite unwell, so I went to the park and sat down on the first seat. With my head in my hands, I told Sue that I was at my wits end and that there was something wrong with me. She got up to go to the ladies and I got up to get a drink from the cafe. Whilst in the cafe, I heard a comment "what's the matter, can't find your bread, mate". I assumed this was a comment from Security Services, expressing their general displeasure with my performance.

When I walked back to the seat, a gentleman was sat there. I thought he was a spy so I approached slowly. He smiled, Then Sue turned up.

On the way back to Exeter, I was still feeling very unwell and I asked to be taken to A&E so I could at least speak to a doctor. The thought that was really bothering me was that I'd somehow been complicit in messing around with the Earth's electromagnetic field so that it broke the weather, causing the damage in Dawlish. That coupled with the thought that government agents were swarming around, that I'd discovered "The Force" and they wanted me to talk to George Lucas about it. Maybe the simple act of putting on the wrong T-shirt was having an effect. I put on my winter top to cover it up, just in case.

Once we were sat in the waiting area, I thought that the government was negotiating with me via the NHS. I thought the people behind me were celebrities who had bought tickets to turn up to the event. The woman opposite was talking into her phone and I thought she was reporting back on what I was doing. So I took my keys out as if to say "who has the keys". I offered them in Sue's direction and got a load of "booing" in response.

Then the woman opposite left and was replaced with a Chinese lad, who had a nasty injury to his shin. I thought this meant that the Chinese government were now the highest bidder for my services. I picked up the magazine next to me and found an article about star signs and the like. I wasn't interested in reading it myself so I offered it to him. I then received comments along the lines of "shock, horror", which sounded like they took all this as an insult.

I got fed up waiting and went back to the reception area. The thing that was bothering me the most at this point was the incident where I'd heard a voice for the first time, saying "Mark" in an Irish accent. The man opposite had a bandaged elbow and I interpreted this as meaning that it was just a flesh wound and I shouldn't worry about it. I've never had such a quick diagnosis from the NHS before or since.

Then a nurse came out and said "Mark Herbert", which sounded like an offer to change my name. She'd come from the direction of the entrance, so I got up and went outside. There was a helicopter on the pad which made it seem like an offer from the military.

Then a man walked past in a Superman costume. In my delusional mind, I heard the comment "you're Superman". That fitted well with my grandiose delusions about myself and made me feel good.

So I was then presented with a choice. Should I become Mark Herbert and go with the military, never seeing my wife and children again. Or should I go back to my life with Sue. It didn't take me long to make up my mind. I walked back inside, told Sue I was feeling better and we left.

On the way back home, we went to mini Tesco's on Cowick Street. There were a number of men waiting outside, talking amongst themselves in an agitated fashion. The delusions continued and I thought they were government agents, displeased with my decision. So I went into the store, took off my winter top, put on my sunglasses and went back outside. In my head, I was sending back the message "mess with me and I'll send the weather in your direction"! They were all taken aback.

When we got back home, the thought that I'd altered the weather by messing with the unified force was deeply implanted in my mind. I started to wonder whether it made any difference which direction I walked in, how fast, whether repeated journeys had a cumulative effect and so on. So I walked around Sanford place and Chieftain Way, in the middle of the road. As I got back towards home, I started to jog, which turned into a run and finally a sprint. I realised I'd finished in the direction of the Sun and threw my arms up in the air. There was a man watching who must have thought I was nuts, but in my mind he watching in admiration.

I walked back into the house. The thought of repeated journeys was hot on my mind so I went inside and traced footsteps around the hall. Then I went into the kitchen and lay down on the ground, face-down with my chest pointing at Mother Earth. After a minute or so, I then turned over and did the same procedure, pointing into the sky.

I can feel a low frequency of some kind <actually it's stopped now>

Seemed like it was coming through the wall.

I thought an earthquake had happened, possibly as a result of my activity.

OK, rather a lot has happened today.

Most significantly I delegated the Mexican Standoff situation to Sue, Claire and my Mum. I won't talk to Claire and my Mum about it. Will just leave it to Sue to sort out.

The negotiation via A&E was I feel necessary to clarify the relationships between Sue and the Medical Profession (at least from my perspective).

Establishing the boundary between A&E and Security Services was also essential from my perspective.

I remain a little perturbed about the meaning of the voice I heard in my head last night. I had to ask the question "Am I Mad' and the answer I'm getting is that we collectively don't know. So we're running on the basis that actually everything is OK here. I will report if I hear any more as I would any other experimental result.

Thank you for the involvement of all the people in Exmouth. I enjoyed that one and I'm pretty sure Sue did too.

Apologies for causing alarm with my behaviour. What is crucial is that I / we gain control of this so that we're all happy that we have levers we can pull in whatever situation arises in future.

So it seems that Gaining Control and Anger Management are related.

I have realised that my anger management is my responsibility. Although I can listen to words of wisdom from you guys and gals, when all is said and done, it's up to me to regain control of myself by whatever means. Clearly this is the part that is causing alarm.

I took on board a lot of rubbish from the experiments on Friday. That required Bowen Therapy and a load of rehydration, which I reported on this morning as part of the room decorating.

I then took on a load more rubbish after the experience with the St Lucia T-Shirt so I get the message that is a particularly sensitive area for you.

Having decided to walk out of the hospital with Sue, I was surprised to be hounded on the way into Tesco's. That was why I put the T-Shirt back on again, and led to the establishment of the Ground Rules.

Followed by Running, so I took the hint that you laid down.

Followed by Sue's suggestion for bare-foot walking on the sand.

This has helped me to feel more connected with the Earth.

I think this is the way to go.

I don't wish to put St Lucia T-Shirt back on again.

I will only do so if you request it.

Unless circumstances push me to a place where I feel I need to go there to gain control once more.

I appreciate that all of this is seriously scary.

I would like to find a way of handing control to you.

From my perspective, I think the most fear comes from the possible association with the weather. Which clearly I don't want to provoke. For what it's worth, my current belief is that if the weather is related to what has gone on, it is more connected to Sue than it is to me.

In terms of running experiments where you pitch my wits against others, I'm happy to do some more of that if you wish.

However, I have a concern for Scott.

Have we checked what the experience was like for him?

Would you like me to do so?

I think we should check that out thoroughly before embarking on any more experiments in that area.

I am assuming you would like me to go to work as normal on Monday.

I have interviews coming up on Tuesday.

Up to you whether you wish to intervene with an alternative agenda here.

I accept this last bit of name-calling in the form of the Baby email.

We all have an element of Adult, Child and Parent in us. In different circumstances, each of these 3 aspects can come out. This does not mean that we Are a Child any more than we Are an Adult. We each have the capability to be each of these in different circumstances.

The reason I thought the weather was associated with Sue was because she'd been camping at Penhalt Farm, Widemouth Bay at the time of the Boscastle disaster. It's just a few miles down the road.

On another occasion, I took a walk down the Riverside Valley Park in the afternoon. It was dry when I headed out. Then an aircraft took off from Exeter Airport just as I was walking back along the 800m stretch of bike path. It started raining quite heavily and as there was strong sunshine from the West, I saw a glorious rainbow in the East.

The rainstorm seemed very localised and synchronous with the plane taking off. All of this made me think that it was a military plane with weather-control seeding technology. I'm pretty sure I didn't hallucinate what actually happened, but my delusion was that the Americans were doing a demo just for me. I certainly didn't believe that I had the power to directly control the weather myself, although I was holding out for the possibility that my work had somehow affected it. My hallucination with the flash of light was driving all of this…

The Rock Gods Came To Topsham

09-03-2014:

My delusions started right after I'd woken up:

At least I assume it was a message.

Felt a disturbance of something through my feet while I was sat on the loo.

Made me tremble for a bit.

And noticed the cats and birds seemed to react at the same time.

Another reference to an earthquake.

Again assuming it was a message.

Was snoozing at the time and it woke me up.

Starting to feel more switched on again but still tired ...

And another.

And the printer has reacted ...

Electrical activity.

More Bowen-style sensations. Twitching. Fingers on right hand got a bit numb. Feeling not-so-switched-on right now...

Bowen Therapy has a habit of doing this, at least with me. Takes me several days to get over it, after which I feel a lot better.

Many years ago, I used to run regularly at lunchtimes with my friend Martin. We would go from work along one of our stock routes, which varied in distance from 3 miles upwards. On one occasion several years ago we'd decided to run to Topsham and back which was 8 miles. On the way back, as it was a sunny day, we decided to explore a path that went along the reed beds, literally right next to the river. We were both seriously taken aback when we encountered a massive seal, together with a bunch of people including the RSPCA, watching from the far side.

We asked what the deal was and they said that it was most likely an old blind seal that had decided for some reason to swim up river and was waiting for the tide to go back again. I'd never been this close to a wild animal like that before and it left a big impression on me.

Winding the clock forward to the present time, the subject of animals was on my mind as I'd been considering relationships between people and it was only natural to ask about them too. This made me think about the seal and I wanted to revisit the place where I'd seen it to pay my respects. So I convinced Sue that we should take a trip to Topsham.

We parked on Holman Way, walked down to The Lighter, upstream past The Passage and onto Topsham Recreation Ground. From there, we continued upstream along the concrete path and onto the reed beds. Sue didn't want to go all the way so did the last bit on my own, the Sun was out.

When I got to the spot, it felt like hallowed ground. So I lay on the ground, chest down to make a strong connection between me and the Earth. Then I turned over and sent a message from me to the sky. Then Sun was out and I imagined making a connection between it and me too. I was praying to the gods.

On the way back, I could hear the sound of cars on the motorway bridge above. I thought the beeping horns were for me.

When we got to The Lighter, I wanted to get a drink so went inside and ordered a bottle of coke. The barman said "thank you sir". I thought this meant I'd been given a knighthood. Then Sue wanted to go to the antiques market so we walked past the people on the tables outside. I thought someone significant was sitting to the left, but was unsure who it was.

Coming out of the antiques market, I'd finished my coke. With my scientific hat on, I knew that glass was made from rock. I walked across and placed my empty bottle on the table. Two men in black leather jackets were seemingly startled by what I'd done and got up. I was convinced they were Phil Collins and Eric Clapton and that I was supposed to find them in some sort of celebrity game. They made the comments "well that's not what I expected" and "I guess it will do". This time I was praying to the rock gods. Maybe they thought that by sending them an empty bottle I was calling them alcoholics.

On the way back to the car, several people walked past and I heard coughs and sneezes. I thought this was their way of apologising for the comments from Phil and Eric.

Excuse me Sir.

For real?

And did I find the Rock Gods?

10-03-2014:

I think Sympathy for the Devil is the right response to that :-)

Loved that song.

Also loved Paint It Black.

Could do with some Satisfaction though ...

Obviously I'd seen something about the Rolling Stones. It seemed the Rock Gods were coming out in force.

Agreed.

Let's make better things for all of us.

Don't recall what I was agreeing to but it sounds quite deep and meaningful

Luscombe Lemonade - Like.

What else do you want me to say here?

Am feeling OK.

This was from a trip to the House of Marbles in the afternoon. I didn't see any more celebrities that day so assume that my delusional state had declined somewhat.

Witches and Cats

Sue always considered herself a white witch, based on her spiritual activities. And she chose 2 black cats, calling them "Sooty" and "Sweep" after the TV show Rainbow. I always got on well with the cats so there was no problem there.

On one occasion, I walked downstairs to find Sweep moving my shoe around with his paw. I'm not sure where this was a hallucination or not, because it came across as "I'd like to walk in your shoes". According to Sue he'd done a similar thing with her shoes, pretending there was a mouse inside, so maybe the cat was the one who was hallucinating.

The general subject of animals was very much on my mind. There had been a string of encounters with animals in the preceding weeks and months:

1.   A porpoise beached on the rocks at Exmouth beach
2.   The seal I'd seen at Topsham years earlier
3.   Swans and ducks swimming alongside
4.   Birds flying past me
5.   Sooty and Sweep doing their thing

Sue always claimed that Sooty and Sweep responded to her and went out into the animal kingdom to do her bidding. By this stage though I was convinced they were responding to me too. In my mind, the porpoise and the seal had taken a journey through the ocean just to see me too. My mind was boggling.

11-03-2014:

PDF Software used for management in government agencies - woohoo!

Wet Floor Sir - acknowledged. Treading carefully here.

Range Credit Card - details in possession.

Two mugs with the cake industry on them - tricky subject.

10 Euro note now in my hands - will deal with this next.

German Trip - am linking this with the 10 Euro note.

Holding 10 Euro note between my hands.

I swapped the 10 Euro note in the kitchen with the box of matches in the lounge. In my head, Sue was now a black witch and was using fire to control her two cats because the matches were next to the cats' toy. Likewise I thought the 10 Euro note signified tensions with Germany since the 2nd World War and the suffering of the Jews in the Holocaust. This was all making me feel quite sick.

Packing In My Job

In essence, my delusions were building up to the point where I was ready to pack in my job, because I thought Google were pulling the strings. This time I was scheduled to meet Sue and her friend Liz for lunch, again at the Waterfront Restaurant. In my crazy head, I took this as a schedule for me to get out of the office by lunchtime. The day started in the gym, where I heard "when news strikes, it strikes fast" on the radio. I was sure this was a sign that they would be reporting my scientific discovery soon.

Sure enough, when Sue drove me to my office, I saw Fiona Bruce waiting to cross the road at the bottom of South Street.

At work, I heard a workman on the scaffolding outside the office say "woohoo". There was no scaffolding. I went out into the stairwell and a man picked up some headphones for a mobile phone, putting them on the handrail. I took this as a sign that I should take them. When I went to the gents, another man in there stared straight at me. I stared back.

Back in the office, I looked outside and there was a group of schoolchildren. I thought they were there to watch when they announced my discovery. I went outside and walked across the quay to the Mace shop. One of the older schoolboys looked straight at me as if the news had been leaked already.

Then the Guardian newspaper sent me an email saying they were in beta test or something like that. I was disappointed because this was a clear sign that they wouldn't be announcing my discovery after all...

So I prepared to clear out of the office. I went and had a one-on-one chat with every developer. And I took all the things out of my drawers, arranging them on my desk in a kind of priority order. I then sat facing each object in turn and made a decision what I was going to do with it. Much of it ended up in the bin, with some items remaining for when I could bring my Land Rover to the car park.

At lunchtime, I went down to the bottom of the stairwell and stepped outside, thinking I would just walk across to the Waterfront. I encountered what I thought were some government agents and a van. I heard the comment "you didn't think you could just doggy-paddle back did you?" This sounded like they were going to give me the run-around and I had to do what they said. So I followed what I thought was the next government agent towards the

Customs House and up the footpath by the city wall. Then across to the top of Friars Gate, where I thought I saw Peter Snow, back down the hill and into the office block by the top entrance, via the car park.

I went back down to the bottom of the stairwell and tried once again to go outside. This time the coast was clear and I met Sue and Liz at the Waterfront.

Sue and Liz sat at a table outside in the sunshine while I went and ordered food at the bar. I was in a delirious state after the events of the morning and was dancing a dance while in the queue. When I got to the bar, I wanted to show a token of faith to my imaginary new employer, so I handed the barman one of my credit cards and asked him to destroy it.

Back outside, I was convinced the people to the left were celebrities talking about us. During the meal, we all ate quietly and the comments stopped. Then once we'd finished, Sue and I were quizzing Liz about various things. She became more and more animated and I heard the comment "they're doing it now". At this point I thought they were referring to mind control and that Sue and I were doing it to Liz. And the strength of the delusion grew to the point where I thought that the whole restaurant was full of celebrities who had bought tickets to watch our show.

Sue and Liz wanted to stay longer, so I said my goodbyes. As I walked between the tables I heard a number of comments about me. As it was still a sunny day, I decided to walk down river.

When I got as far as the Port Royal, the man on the nearest bench said "fuck off, this one's ours". I stopped abruptly as this seemed like a boundary that I'd crossed. In my mind, the Port Royal was full of Security Services staff while The Waterfront was full of celebrities. So I turned around and walked back, bumping into Sue and Liz on the way. They decided to walk with me and as we passed The Waterfront I heard "shocking, absolutely shocking". I thought this meant we had to go inside and introduce ourselves, but as Sue and Liz were in charge this was out of the question.

When we got to the other side of Cricklepit Bridge, Sue and Liz turned down river once more while I carried on up, towards St Thomas.

At the Riverside junction, I walked across the road. The man in the car to the right was taking his penis out of his trousers and giving it a jerk, suggesting to me that he thought I was a wanker. I also heard some shouting so I interpreted this as crossing the Security Services boundary once again. In my mind, the flow of cars was staffed by agents who were all part of a massive security operation to protect the celebrities.

Not wanting to upset them any more than I had to, I ran the rest of the way home. Then got into Mandy the Landy and drove back to work. All the way there I was conscious of who was in the other cars.

When I got there, the entrance to the car park was blocked by a van unloading. So I parked in the one of the spaces opposite knowing that I wouldn't be long. I noticed the sign on the gate with said "Secure Force UK". In my mind, this meant that my imaginary new employer, which I assumed was Google, had taken delivery of the unified force and now owned the whole thing.

After that I went down into the office to pick-up my things. On the trip back up to the Land Rover I encountered a man on a motorcycle. He smiled through his helmet. I thought he was Gordon Ramsay.

And then I took a few unscheduled days off work …

The TV Was Talking To Me

I'd been following people around on the streets outside thinking that they were government agents. This had been going on for some time and it kind of came to a head one lunchtime when I went upstairs into the lounge with Sue.

In my warped belief system, I was assigning electromagnetic force values to physical objects in my possession. And I was imagining that this had an impact on my environment when I pushed the object in one direction or the other. For documents, the information they contained could be transmitted into the Earth either by lying on it with my chest, or sitting on it with my backside.

On this occasion there were some documents that I gathered together and placed by chair by the desk, ready for transmitting to Mother Earth. And there was my chess set (which I'd made myself many years earlier) on the foot stool in front of the sofa. I chose to sit on the sofa, behind the chess set, watching TV.

The show was hosted by Alexander Armstrong, I can't remember which show exactly, but I remember a sense of him talking to me personally, that when he looked into the camera, he was looking at me and so on. He commented that the board was stacked in my favour, which I took to be a reference about the chess board. After a while, my grandiose delusion had taken over and I was being credited with having discovered the unified force. There was a discussion about email addresses and domain names ending in .tv for television and the fact that this also stood for Tuvalu. Which by the way is the format used by my employer. Alexander made some comment about me getting a whole island the size of Tuvalu in return for what I had done.

At that point, things started to get a little crazy and I had what I believe to be my first visual hallucination. I saw a woman with dark hair on the lower right of the TV screen, in a kind of separate frame on her own. She was staring at the screen as if waiting for a response. I smiled and she smiled back. I then pushed out my chest to send an electromagnetic pulse and she was delighted, almost getting out of her chair.

The game show finished and with it the hallucination. It was followed by a sitcom, where they were discussing getting me to go outdoors. Sue was sat on the sofa opposite me with seemingly no interest in going anywhere. So I got up and sat on the other end of her sofa, then intention being to stir up the electromagnetic force to encourage Sue to come with me.

Sue took the invitation and we left the house together, walking down the street hand-in-hand.

She left to go to the St Thomas shops while I carried on up to town. By this point, the government agents had turned out in force and it was an easy matter for me to follow some of them from a distance.

Once in town, I spent the next hour or so following people around with crazy things going on in my head. Eventually I became exhausted and had to get a drink from a supermarket, at which point the overall delusion came to an end.

Diagnosed With Bipolar Disorder

In the run up to diagnosis, my behaviour was becoming more and more erratic. One Saturday, at the start of a week off, I went out for a lads' night out with the neighbours. This turned out to be a mistake because we'd agreed to go on a pub crawl "The St Thomas Ten". The list of pubs was to be made up as we went along, starting with the Sawyers Arms, the General Buller and the Kings. The Kings was by far the most animated of these, with a live band later in the evening. Nevertheless we pressed on, going to the night club in the old St Thomas Railway Station building. That was empty bar two girls dancing in the middle, so we then went on to the Royal Oak Inn.

We stayed for two pints and then it was decision time. Should we carry on in the general direction of the Green Gables, or go back to the Kings. There was some distinct homophobic sentiment in the pub, with the Green Gables reputed to be a gay pub, but in the end the decisive factor was the live band in the Kings. So we decided to go back.

By the time we got back to the Kings, I'd had way too much already. One pint was quite enough for me, two would have been a night out on the town so to have six pints and counting was just madness. Not only that, I think I had two more at the Kings before staggering home.

I lost Sunday entirely to illness. What I didn't realise was the extent to which the alcohol would fuel my delusions over the next few days

On Monday I went for a bike ride to Turf Locks, wearing my green cycling top which made me think I was Google's Android. I thought I was demonstrating my capabilities to government agents along the way. Just past the Swing Bridge, I thought I saw ex-president Bill Clinton. At that point I thought it had turned into a military exercise and sure enough within half a mile I saw two military men walking the opposite way. One of them said "you don't need to slow down for us, mate". To this day, I will never know whether this was a hallucination or not.

As I approached Turf Locks, there were construction vehicles and piles of gravel. I thought this meant I was leaving the safe zone and was on my own, out in the wilderness. This spurred me on to increase my effort and I went whizzing along until I got to the lock gate. I put my bike on my shoulder, crossed the lock gate and put it in the hedge. At that point, I spotted some twigs on the ground which seemed to be leading to the far end. I followed them, pushing the larger ones to the side to clear the path. I thought I was following a trail laid by the military and that this was all part of the exercise. When I got to the far end, I stripped off and went for a swim. It was February!

The cold water was enough to calm my mood and the delusions settled down. The way back was relatively uneventful, although I passed a crowd of people on the 800m stretch by the flood plain and thought they were cheering me on. Then there were some swans on the narrow path with tons of pedestrians so I had to slow down. Then I clocked another pair of swans were swimming in tandem. They seemed like a couple and I thought they had come out to see me. Then I saw a pair of ducks and the delusion intensified. At this point, the whole animal kingdom understood what was going on.

Once I got back, there was a pile of garden rubbish that needed taking to the Recycling Centre. I was wearing my blue micro-fleece from Go Outdoors and thought I was Obi-Wan Kenobi.

Then I drove round to the crematorium to spend some time at Thomas's grave. There was a funeral service about to start in chapel and I ran in, bursting into tears. Needless to say I was asked to leave. I think that my thoughts and feelings at that point were genuine grief for Thomas, though I'd never expressed it in such an outward way before.

On Tuesday I decided to go to Marsh Barton to look at cars. The Google Android persona was firmly implanted in my head, even though I was walking and not cycling this time. I'd also made the connection with my Google Nexus phone and thought that Google were on the end of it. When the symbol for voice control came up, I thought they were listening to me and so I chatted away with whatever came up.

I walked up to the BMW garage and asked to speak to a salesman. I remember waiting for 20 minutes, reading magazines, drinking water and watching the other customers who were sat there. The salesman became available and I sat down at his desk. During the discussion, apparently I lied and told him I'd been working for Siemens for 22 years. I don't remember this, but he reported it to Sue when she spoke to him later. I had actually worked there for 18 months after university so maybe the German connection was driving my misrepresentation of the facts. I was certainly thinking about BMW as a German company on the end of the line of car companies on the way out of Marsh Barton towards Matford Roundabout. The thought that was really bothering me was that the Jaguar and Aston Martin garage was on the opposite side of the road, representing England. And that if you drew a line extrapolating out from Bad Homburg Way, you got to Dawlish where the damage to the sea wall had been done. Was it possible that the electromagnetic energy represented by international tensions had planted itself in the ground and was affecting the weather? Exeter after all was the location where my vision regarding the unified force had taken place.

I went outside and gave a description of what I could see to Google. Starting with the park and ride, then across to the cattle market and finally opposite a sign which said "Secure Force". It was the same security firm as used at my place of work. Someone slammed a car boot at that point, which I took as an acknowledgement from Security Services.

We then went on a test drive in a BMW Z4. I really enjoyed driving it up the A38 as far as Chudleigh. The windy stretch on the way back to the top of Haldon Hill was great, although the salesman had to caution me because I was doing 100mph. When we got back, I said that I liked at and went inside to place an order. There was no way I could afford £600 a month to buy a new car like that, but in my delusional state, Google were paying the bill so it didn't matter. In reality, I paid the deposit from our joint bank account and set up direct debit from that account. This was a classic manic purchase.

I then went for lunch at the Carriages Devon Hotel which was just a short walk away, leaving my payment card at the BMW garage. When I got to Matford Roundabout, I lay down on the grass and listened to the cars passing by on all sides. I imagined that this was stirring up my electromagnetic energy in a healthy way, particularly with lorries headed for the Recycling Centre with a full load of rubbish. I also watched a plane fly overhead and thought that the passengers had volunteered take away my excess energy.

When I got to the hotel, I ordered food and drink at the bar and then sat alone, at a table outside in the sunshine while everyone else was inside. I was feeling particularly good with myself and basically thought I was The Stig from Top Gear. If my job was to review cars, then the next stop was the Jaguar / Aston garage, but first I was going to continue my walk in the direction of Dawlish by going up Old Matford Lane. I went back inside the hotel and a woman said "we're going on a trip", which I imagined as a rocket ship to Mars. I went into the other room where a project manager was showing his work to a client. I introduced myself and said I was a project manager too, albeit in IT. This was about the only thing I'd said all day which wasn't delusional, though it is very unlikely I would have introduced myself had I not been in a manic state.

I walked up Old Matford Lane, stopped for the view across Marsh Barton and then continued towards Exminster, where I used to live, so I was familiar with the territory. When I crossed the motorway bridge, I encountered a woman with her dogs, except that the dogs were in the lane while she was doing stuff in the field. I stopped to ask if everything was OK, then continued down the Deepway Lane hill. One of the dogs decided to follow me and try as a might, I couldn't get it to go back. In my crazy head, this was another sign that my electromagnetic energy was very high. The dog followed me all the way to Tesco's, where I asked one the assistants to take the dog off me. They agreed to return it to the owner. After this I headed back, having taken enough of a trip in the direction of Dawlish.

Having got back to the Devon Hotel, I then took the short walk back down the other side of Bad Homburg way to Jaguar / Aston Martin. I noted a parked pickup truck which had a load of rubbish in the back. It left straight away, which I imagined as removing more excess electromagnetic energy from the scene.

When I went inside, I wasn't able to convince them to let me have a test drive in an Aston Martin. So the discussion moved onto deep and meaningful things, spurred onto their poster about helping the environment. This tallied with my ongoing obsession with the damage done to the Dawlish sea wall. The salesman even involved the senior manager given the level of interest I was showing in their policy. We all said "mmm" a number of times and nodded heads in agreement. I have no idea whether they thought I was delusional or not. To this day, I believe that my behaviour was perfectly plausible as an Aston Martin customer, but we would have to ask them to find out for real.

After that, it was back to the BMW garage which was a short hop across Bad Homburg Way. I retrieved my payment card and went home.

According to Sue, I then had a doctor's appointment and given my general behaviour, it was agreed that the Crisis Team would visit me every day. I don't recall this, although I do remember their visiting the house on at least one occasion.

Apparently I was doing daft things like leaving the door open and going out picking litter. More than likely, I was following trails on the ground thinking they'd been left there by the military.

On Saturday evening, I remember going out and there being a man leaning out of the upper floor window looking at me. This was the first time the government had seemingly asked me a direct question and he said "how long are you going to keep this up for". I gulped and looked back at him in amazement because I thought I was doing OK. In any case they'd already had plenty of opportunities to intervene and actually talk to me. I said "can I just go to the pub, please". He briefly asked his house mate and recommended the General Buller. I have absolutely no idea whether his initial comment to me was a hallucination or not. I would make sense if it was.

I went to the General Buller and there were two men at the bar. I imagined these were government agents, checking to make sure the barmaid was safe in my presence. After a while, they left one by one and I had a nice time chatting to the barmaid. It didn't occur to me that I was married and that this was not really an appropriate thing to be doing. I thought that the music playing was the government trying to talk to me. They were playing Comfortably Numb by Pink Floyd.

I went back home and had a bath. However, I stayed there so long that Sue burst in and pulled the plug out. I was outraged and Sue fled the bathroom. She phoned the police and a policeman arrived to talk to me by the time I'd got dressed. He discussed my behaviour, which to be honest I thought was reasonable. Nevertheless he insisted I slept somewhere else that night so I checked into the Great Western Hotel. I didn't relish this because it reminded me of the time before when I spent money on a string of hotels, but given it was the police there was little I could do.

On Sunday, I went round to my mother's for tea. Then the Crisis Team turned up. Theo had been briefed on what had happened and got me to agree to come into hospital voluntarily. We drove directly to The Cedars mental hospital.

When I got there and settled into my new room, Sue, bless her, had found the BMW receipt and phoned them up to cancel the order for the car. I remember being particularly annoyed that she had done so. I told her that meant she could kiss goodbye to her Aston Martin, which I thought would also be paid for by Google. Clearly my delusions were running away with me, which shows how much I needed anti-psychotic medication.

The following day I was diagnosed with Bipolar Disorder. I was put on Lithium Carbonate as a mood stabiliser and Olanzapine as an anti-psychotic.

Detained Under Section 2

Back in the community, I wasn't getting on at all well with Olanzapine. It was having a depressant effect on me and as someone with depressive tendencies, that wasn't a good thing. Also I was having a hard time coming to terms with my diagnosis. It was one thing being diagnosed with depression (unipolar disorder) 15 years previously, but bipolar disorder was something else entirely. My self-esteem had taken a real knock.

I remember having frequent thoughts of suicide. I'd thought about jumping off a bridge, and checked out the one across the A30 on the way to Shillingford St George. In the event, I was scared of heights and didn't have the courage to go through with it. Then I thought about the railway line and checked out the foot crossing near the canal. Despite several attempts to hang around there, I didn't have the courage to go through with that either. I even went to the level crossing at Stoke Canon, but that was way too fast and scary.

I talked about the Olanzapine with my NHS care coordinator and the message got back to the consultant, who changed my prescription from Olanzapine to Quetiapine. The idea was that Quetiapine had an anti-depressant effect and that would be a better match for me. However, I was shocked for 2 reasons:

1. They were planning on making the switch while I was out in the community, whereas I'd spent several weeks in hospital getting used to Olanzapine
2. They didn't tell me how much of a sedative effect it had

I took the prescribed dose and after a few days it was an absolute joke. I was practically asleep on my feet. When I woke up one morning, my mood was so low that banged my head on a geode on the windowsill. And I took a knife into the bathroom with me. I remember going down to the river bank just up from the Mill On The Exe and sleeping for a couple of hours before midday.

Then we were booked to go a wedding party that afternoon and evening which we did, with me having woken up by then. I was quiet, but otherwise OK at this point.

The following morning I was in a real mess. The sedative effect of the Quetiapine was weighing heavily on my mind and I ended up having an argument with Sue.

I got into the car and was about to drive off into oblivion when Sue got in next to me. All I could think about was driving to the railway crossing at Powderham as that was one I hadn't tried.

On the way, Sue was on the phone to the authorities. First the Crisis Team I think and then the police.

When I got there, I parked up and walked straight up onto the railway line and sat down. As luck would have it, a train was coming straight away, albeit on the other line. Sue and a complete stranger made a heroic effort to drag me off the line.

Still not satisfied, I then thought that I would swim off into oblivion. So I crossed the line, stripped down to my underpants and started to swim across the River Exe.
It was very calm and cool in the water. Rather than swim out to sea, my plan was seemingly to get to the other side. When I got about half way I thought better of it and turned back.

On arrival back, a policeman was waiting on the mud. I collected my things and agreed to go with him. A team of railway police were waiting by the line, They moved back to the roadside as I crossed the line and reported this back on the radio. When I reached the police van, I was detained under Section 2.

This time it stuck and from memory I was in for a 6-week stay in The Cedars. At least it gave them time to put me properly on Quetiapine starting with 150mg and working up to 300mg. To this day, I maintain that the sedative effects are too much though. I just about got used to it, but when I was released from hospital the temptation to reduce the dose was immense. This was basically a ticking time bomb for the next stress-related episode.

Violent Behaviour

Summer 2014 was a relatively quiet time as far as I can recall. I think there may have been one more voluntary admission to hospital because I can remember Sue turning up one day with body boards so we could spend the day out at Widemouth Bay. She was absolutely brilliant at doing things like that and that was one of the reasons why I loved her so much.

Our relationship deteriorated after that.

In September, Sue said that she wanted a separation, for me to move out into rented accommodation. I was upset about that. She wasn't basing it so much on what had happened recently but going back to the hurtful email I'd sent in January.

Things didn't improve in October and the arguments continued. This set the stage for the worst behaviour I have ever displayed. I am absolutely ashamed about what happened so am writing this with apprehension.

We woke up one morning and Sue gave me a rapid-fire dump of all the things that were bothering her. I can't remember what it was all about specifically, but something along the lines of wanting to end our relationship. There was some element of what she said that made me really angry though. I can remember that.

We went downstairs and I ate my breakfast. The argument continued and I was so outraged that I stood up and poured the remains of my cereal bowl onto her head. I then slapped her on both cheeks and had several more attempted slaps in a kind of tussle, catching her arms in the process.

Still angry I went outside, then started to empty the contents of her Bowen Therapy room into my Land Rover. Apparently the logic here is that when someone like me is presented with a rejection, they make the decision that nobody else should have them either. I wasn't aware of why I was doing what I was doing, it just seemed like the next thing to do. I didn't realise that this was the last time I would see or be able to communicate with Sue for 6 months.

When I got to the Recycling Centre, I thought better of it and turned around. When I got back to the house, the police were waiting for me and I never got a chance to unload.

A passer-by had photographed what was going on his phone and the police thought they had enough to prosecute without Sue, so they arrested me.

I spent the rest of the day in a police cell, feeling absolutely awful.

They released me on bail, pending a court hearing the following Monday.

My life had ended.

Committed Suicide

I went to stay at a cheap hotel in Sidmouth. I knew the routine from before and thought that I would most likely end up at Globe Backpackers for a while. That was without any knowledge of what was about to happen next.

I went to sleep thinking I would have a nice day in Sidmouth, by the sea. However, I woke up in an altogether different mood, feeling utterly suicidal. After breakfast, I wandered up the street not knowing what I was going to do, until I reached a petrol station. Then the thought of setting fire to myself on Woodbury Common took hold. So I went back, bought a lighter in a supermarket, got the car, drove to the petrol station and bought a can full of petrol.

On Woodbury Common, I took the can with me down to a quiet spot next to water, so I didn't set fire to the whole common. I stripped off and was contemplating pouring the petrol over myself, when a positive thought ran through my head regarding my children. So I phoned the Crisis Team and explained what had happened. They told me to take the petrol can back to the garage, which I did. Then I went back to the hotel. Once again I'd failed to step up to the mark.

That thought kept going round and round in my head while I was in the hotel room. I looked at the stack of pills and decided to take an overdose. Having already researched it, I knew that 25x 300mg Quetiapine should be enough, so if I took 50 then there should be no doubt. I broke them up into bits and swallowed the lot.

After a while I decided to go outside and staggered up the street becoming less and less conscious. I made it as far as the petrol station and had a change of heart. I didn't want to go through with it and please would they call an ambulance.

As it was Sidmouth, the ambulance came all the way from Exeter and took an age to arrive. I just about held it together by sitting on the wall.

When the ambulance arrived, I was able to get inside. I sat quietly for the journey.

When we got to A&E, I just about remember getting out of the ambulance. After that I was unconscious.

I woke up in intensive care, surprised to be alive. I tried talking to the nurses, but with all the medical equipment surrounding me and the fact that I was still hung over from the Quetiapine, it was impossible. I remember feeling utterly helpless. I was also concerned about going to the loo, not knowing they already had that covered with a tube in my penis.

After a while, maybe a day or so, I started to come round and they took off the bits of medical equipment. I sat in the chair for a while.

Then I was summoned to talk to the consultant. He knew about the setting fire incident from the Crisis Team report and said there was a great amount of anger in me. He also said he doubted my bipolar diagnosis but didn't say what he had in mind instead. He asked if I knew what the date was and I said no. He said I'd been unconscious for 3 days.

After this, I was checked into The Cedars for another stay in mental hospital. This time, the main topic was where I was going to live. They were adamant that they didn't want me to live in a string of hotels or be on the street. So they hunted around for another solution. In the event, my mother stepped up to the mark and offered for me to stay round at her place. At least until I was well enough to get a place of my own.

I don't recall whether I had any specific delusions or hallucinations during this time but it's highly likely. Essentially I found out that 300mg Quetiapine is not enough to stop psychosis, given sufficient levels of stress. This, coupled with the fact that it was still having a sedative effect on me, set the stage for another episode of manic behaviour.

Criminal Conviction

Once I'd got out of hospital, I had to face up to the charges that were levied against me. My NHS care coordinator did a sterling job of helping me through the process, having been a probation officer himself in a former life.

I was ready to face the charges in court and turned up at the relevant time. I received 2 major surprises:

1. A bailiff turned up to serve me with a Non-Molestation Order that had been taken out by Sue, as advised by the police
2. I was arrested for breach of the terms of that order for messages I'd posted on my Facebook wall

So I spent another day in a police cell, this time staying the night too while they rescheduled my court appearance for the following day. At least they agreed the breaches of the order were mild and that I had no idea it had been taken out, having been served with it only minutes beforehand.

This gave me time to speak to a criminal lawyer and he handled the court appearance itself. Essentially another court date was booked where I would be sentenced. In the meantime I had to chat with the probation service so they could write a report.

When it came to the hearing, it was delayed until the afternoon. I was finally given a Conditional Discharge, given my previous good behaviour. There was no supervision required because I was already under the care of the NHS.

Some time passed before I was arrested again, this time for a more obvious breach of the Non-Molestation Order. I had been attending salsa classes on a Monday evening, at the Moose Hall, which was where Sue and I had gone on a number of occasions. Sue was nowhere in sight so I assumed it was safe to carry on going there. Then one evening, I paid the fee for the class, put my shoes on and was shocked to see Sue there. Not knowing what to do for the best, I decided to carry on with the class, given that it was the shines format and we would be dancing alone.

When it came to the end of the class, I went to the teacher, Angus and asked him to ask Sue if it was OK for me to attend the following class, given that we would be dancing together. The message came back that there was a legal issue. I took this as a "no" so packed up and left.

Several day later, on Saturday evening, I was about to go out to dinner with my mum and Pete when I was visited by the police. They said it would be just some questions but I knew the drill. I was taken to Heavitree Police Station once more, arrested and placed in a cell. By this stage I was beginning to think this was more of a farce than anything else, though not wanting to stay the night in the cell again. However, I should give the police some credit because they'd organised it so that I would be questioned right away. The fact that they'd left it a few days before arresting me gave an indication of the level of concern they had and although the questions were pointed, I was able to answer them with ease.

I was taken back to the cell, then ten minutes later I was freed. The duty sergeant took the view that I'd behaved entirely reasonably and that there was no prospect of a conviction.

Some weeks passed, during which my general delusional state increased. Clearly the legal process had taken a toll on my levels of stress. Then I made the mistake of reducing my levels of Quetiapine from 300mg to 100mg because I was fed up with the sedation. I also told my NHS care coordinator, which turned out to be a mistake because it gave the NHS an excuse to tinker with my medication once more.

Poems By Sue

Poem #1:
Thrown down the stairs, all piles of glass
Who knew this marriage wouldn't last
It was only Christmas a few days ago
But already issues and tales of woe
I've been here for you, staying strong
But it's all my fault whatever went wrong
When will you look and see who you are
Bully to me, threatened by my car
How did I miss all of the signs
Obvious now by your solicitors lines
I thought you loved me, how stupid of me
Why has it taken so long for me to see
Apparently it's my issues that caused all the mess
Now I have freedom I feel truly blessed
No worries or headaches about what I do
Hopefully you will be feeling it too
The police got involved to protect myself
Laughable really, now you are after my wealth
Oh what a sad sorry affair,
Let's say its time, I am very aware.
When meeting in future another man
I certainly won't have or want a marriage plan
Happy, healthy and single I am
It's better than a marriage that's only a sham
I'm not sure I ever really knew who you were
The four or so years passed in a quick firing blur
One thing I say after all of this
Is a glass of fruit cider alone is absolute pure bliss

Poem #2:
Here I am left all alone.
You're not allowed to contact me, text or phone.
What did I do to bring all this on
Find my voice, the words to my song
It went on too long, almost two years,
Having to deal with your angst and all of your fears.
You told me it was them that caused all the rust.
Told me your tales and as a good wife I trust.
I honoured your body, believed your big lie.
Now time out and the untruths multiply.
What did I do to deserve all of this.
Complexity of duplicity, everything amiss.

I trusted completely, just like a fool.
I lived like I needed to obey a big rule.
Now I have freedom to look and reflect.
It was like living without honour in a weird sexual sect.
Now you have no power, your control all gone.
It's my assets you're after, it didn't take long.
Your secrets out, I can see who you are.
You can force my hand but you won't get far.
For I promise you this from the heart of my soul.
It will eat you up like a great burning hole,
Whatever you do without honour and respect.
At the end of the day, it's on you that it will reflect.

Poem #3:
I pulled you off the railway line, as the train was coming near.
With the help of a passer-by, us both ignoring fear.
You fought us off to go for a muddy estuary swim.
We stood on the railway side watching you following your whim.
After you emerged they sectioned you, any thoughts of others
never on view.
How I felt about what you did, I kept inside so you never knew.
Shocking it was to experience that,
Sat at home alone crying with two cats on my lap.
Only six months later and after all I went through.
To our verbal and written agreements you're not being true.
I brought up your children just like my own.
Cooked, washed their clothes, hugged and provided a home.
The biggest sadness in all of this .
Was the hope and goodwill of our very first kiss.
Now is the time for me to heal and move on.
I sometimes wonder if you're at all sorry now you're gone.
After you beat me, your arrest, it all.
That evening about me, you put insults on your face book wall.
Shocked and in horror, a week later I saw.
Your demands in face book ink, more of what you put before.
Goodbye to you as I now move along.
I am looking forward to my newly emerging song.
I miss the kids, but that's how it is.
The rest is perfect, nothing but peaceful bliss.

Messages Received

09-03-2015:

I was feeling good about myself in March 2015, in spite of the criminal conviction in December and the ongoing divorce proceedings. I had absolutely no idea that this meant manic behaviour was creeping up on me and with it psychosis too.

It all started when I considered the earlier episode, where the government was supposedly reading my emails and sending agents my way. What if it was true after all and I'd missed out due to my mental health issues? A whole year had gone by since then.

If this was the case then there was still a sale to be made based on the work I had put in. Accordingly I started to write "Messages Received" emails from me to me, hoping that this would be the signature for them to pay attention.

Took the Henry VIII quote off POF.

And avoided the obstacles you place in my way.

Let's do it.

I will go work for the American Military, assuming they're the highest bidder in all of this.

Please look out for my children. I'm sure you will.

Clearly I will find it v. Hard to deal with if I don't get to see them any more. Not to mention the effect it will have on them.

I'd been dating, hence the comment about Plenty Of Fish. My profile had said something like "Divorced the first wife and beheaded the second, who wants to be number three?" In retrospect and given my criminal conviction, I thought that maybe they wouldn't see the funny side of this. I didn't seriously believe I was Henry VIII reincarnated, so my psychosis clearly had some limits.

Whereas I seriously thought the American Military were interested in my physics work.

10-03-2015:

Various ... many from the office this morning.

TNT, it's an option.

I'd like to go for a drive to Dawlish at lunchtime.

Whether either of these are a good idea is another thing ...

I assume that my entire life, who I meet, whatever else I do is completely controlled by you.
Not much fun really.

Marmaris. Just a holiday really.

The previous holiday had been a self-catering hotel in Majorca, which worked really well, except for the fact that Claire didn't want to carry on with buying food, cooking etc. as would be the case at home. On the one hand, this was a trap she set for herself because she refused to let me do anything in the kitchen right from the outset of our relationship. On the other hand, I can understand that she wanted a break and something different when we went on holiday. Majorca was reasonably economical, though I had booked it via a high street travel agent, can't remember which one.

So the next time I booked online to reduce the price, and then spent the difference on upgrading to all-inclusive. Great hotel in Marmaris, Grand hotel something?? Sunny and v.hot in July. Loved the pool, water slide for the kids and the access to the sea, admittedly without much of a beach. I swam out to the diving platform many times and by the end of the week had the kids doing the same. Claire stayed by the pool. And didn't sleep with me once. This was the end of it really. I don't know what her problem was. Sue reckoned she'd been unfaithful early on and the guilt was eating into her. This could be Sue's fears talking here though ... I suspect losing Thomas was a v.large part of it. Or maybe it was just me ... who knows. Anyway, I do remember running in the evening, in the dark at 9pm to keep the temperature down as much as possible. Then jumping in the sea in the pitch dark, only to find there was a couple there enjoying an intimate moment. Whoever you were ... I'm sorry for ruining it for you :-) It was kind of funny though.
The TNT comment was in response to a large van that was parked outside the office.

Marmaris was in response to me walking down Western Road in Exeter where my father used to work. This was the name of one of the houses.

The subject of weather control was on my mind, hence the comment about Dawlish...

Trippy Stuff Around The River Exe

Thinking back to a year earlier, I could remember the subject of weather control. I also remembered my ideas about a line of force running from Marsh Barton down to the Dawlish Sea Wall, which suffered severe weather damage in the storms of January 2014.

I also considered the number of times I'd been to Exmouth and Dawlish Warren, which were favourite places of mine on either side of the River Exe. What if there was some connection between my activities, the river and the weather? I'd even built a model railway which included a section that looked like the red cliffs from the Dawlish-Teignmouth section, so it seemed that a lot of my energy was focussed there.

One evening, I got in my Mazda MX5. This was probably a manic purchase, from the Ivybridge Trade Centre, after dating a woman from Ivybridge, but that's another story.

I drove to Orcambe Point, parked up, walked around the beach for a bit, followed some footprints in the sand and encountered a woman walking her dog. Then I walked up to the monument at the end, weaving in and out of the columns. Satisfied that I'd left enough of an imprint at Exmouth I got back in my car.

I stopped at the Shell garage on Countess Wear roundabout. Not sure where I was going next, I walked inside. Then I thought of Dawlish Warren and bought a torch. I stopped at the Countess Wear lodge to get a drink before heading off.

When I got there, I parked up and walked out onto the beach. After countless groins and a long section of sand at the end of the spit, I reached the spot opposite Exmouth. I then stripped off down to my underpants and went for a paddle. I reasoned it was probably too dangerous to go for a swim given the darkness and the likely river currents.

After this, I went back, drove to Dawlish past the site of sea wall damage and turned around underneath the cliff with the railway tunnel. Satisfied that I'd left enough of an imprint in Dawlish / Warren I headed back towards Exeter.

For some reason, I decided to stop at The Anchor in Cockwood. After getting a drink, I walked to the far end and was about to go upstairs when I heard "That was a fucking tremor". In my crazy belief system, controlling the weather turned into setting off earthquakes.

I sat and watched some guys playing darts while I finished my drinks. Only by this stage I was terrified about driving back across the river along Bridge Road in case something else happened.

So I headed further up river. Eventually I got to Crediton, at which point I felt it was safe enough to give it a go. So I took the road to Tiverton. This was not a road I was familiar with and was surprised with the number of twists and turns, ups and downs. On the higher ground it became quite foggy and this scared me a little in case I'd caused that too.

Finally I crossed the River Exe at Bickleigh and absolutely nothing happened. Only this time I became convinced that I was still in a toxic state as a result of what I'd done and needed to detox somehow.

When I got to the turning for Thorverton, I took it knowing there was a bridge over the river. I drove up to it, parked, got out and walked to the middle. After a bit I thought I saw lights going out in the village. And had a vision of fire engines running around, but I'm pretty sure I didn't actually see any. After a while, I felt better and decided it was safe to go home. It was nearly midnight by the time I got back.

Madonna Wanted To Marry Me

11-03-2015:

You wish. Think we can all share in that one.

Great if you've got nothing better to do. This is what I do.

Nasty stary woman. Who was she??

The skateboarder ... really appreciate. Please thank him from me.

Sale agreed ... my choice. Understood.

Start a war. WTF?

There was another big message, but I've forgotten what it was. Sorry.

Find my name. Done.

Mark = Mars = Roman god of war, we all know that.

Mansfield. Well that's Sue's tribal name isn't it. The decision to change my name was something that seemed like the right thing to do at the time. Interestingly, many women I've spoken to about it really like the idea. I guess because it goes against the grain of established tradition and puts them first for a change. The receptionist at Rundle Walker (in the old office before they moved), she liked it. And so did the clerk at Nat West bank.

Go to Honiton. Was she planted by you?

Go to Totnes. Was she planted by you too?

What about the next one??

I guess this comes down to who has what information.

The nasty stary woman was on the quay after Jack and I had returned from a 6-mile run to Ide and back that we called "The Shopping Run".

The skateboarder went down the middle of Bridge Street on his chest as I was walking along. I thought he'd done it just for me.

The other big message was a woman who I'd thought was Julia Roberts on Fore Street.

The women from Honiton and Totnes were dates in February. I was obviously sensitive to messages containing those names.

Of all these, the biggest message was the nasty stary woman, because I thought she looked like Madonna. Also, she was staring right at me whereas Julia Roberts was walking away. Accordingly I looked up Madonna tracks when I was in the office with some free time that evening. You can tell that all the pieces were in place for a manic episode complete with hospitalisation because there were no more "Messages Received" after this. Doing it for just 2 days was enough to bring on psychosis and at a level way beyond what I'd experienced before.

The first track I searched for was "Into The Groove". I was immediately struck by the opening where she says "Good going stranger". I thought she was talking to me and that this was a live video, in spite of knowing deep down that it was originally recorded in the 1980s. Then there was a reference to "Desperately Seeking Susan" with an ad in the newspaper. This blew me away because I thought she was making a disparaging comment on my dating efforts up to that point. Finally, the video contained several shots of a photographer with a flash gun, pointing directly at the camera. That merely served to reinforce my delusion that they were taking photos of me while I was watching the video. In my crazy head, all of this meant that Madonna fancied me and wanted me to chase her instead. I must admit I felt guilty because I'd spent much of my youth listening to Blondie.

Clearly I had forgotten that "Desperately Seeking Susan" was a movie starring Madonna. Either that or I never knew it in the first place. Or maybe my mind was selectively forgetting it because it suited my delusion. Either way, the next thing I searched for was another Madonna track. The trouble is I have no recollection which one it was. Maybe it was the next link on YouTube. What I do remember is thinking that the video was live with Madonna performing in a frame for me and me alone, but surrounded by other bits of video which were recorded. Accordingly, when the video was done, I sat at my computer and spoke my feedback to the screen, convinced that she could both see and hear what was going on. I told her that it was confusing, not knowing which bits were live and which were not.

The next video I saw was Madonna being taken away in an ambulance. Again I have no idea which video it was. Maybe I hallucinated the whole thing. Effectively I was being told that my comments were not well received and she'd been taken ill as a result.

She obviously recovered quickly because I was able to watch the next video straight away. It was an improvement on the last because it had Madonna live in full frame. Again I don't remember which one it was, my best guess is "Express Yourself". The part that had the most effect on me was when Madonna thrust her chest out. That literally knocked me back in my chair. And then she did a similar move with her hips that caused me laser-like pain in my groin. I can say that from experience because I had a vasectomy via that method many years ago. All of this convinced me that Madonna had been trained in the ways of The Force and knew a thing or two that I didn't!

I watched "Into The Groove" once more and this time through I noticed a man sawing wood, which reminded me of "cutting through issues" and a hotel room door with the number 1313 on it. This suggested to me that she was in a hotel somewhere and I needed to find her…

The next day, Madonna was still on my mind. Without knowing where she would be, I thought the obvious thing to do was to visit Timepiece, the night club in the middle of Exeter. With my crazy unified force leather jacket on, I decided to take a somewhat circuitous route to get there. I would be going around the Roman City Wall, starting at the Water Gate corner down on the quay. I walked up the hill, over the bridge, past South Gate, along the path, into Southernhay, into Princesshay across the high street and down the passageway next to Boots.

When I popped out onto Bailey Street, I had a strong desire to go into Harry's Bar and Grill on the off-chance Madonna was in there. I ordered a non-alcoholic mojito cocktail and sat down on the sofa in the room to the right. For some reason the arrangement of chairs bothered me so I moved them all around. Then sat there playing a game of chess on my Google Nexus phone, listening to the music they were playing in the bar. I played the best game of chess I'd ever done, managing to beat the computer with a king's knight opening, albeit on level one. And I thought the music was talking to me.

When I'd finished my cocktail and it was clear Madonna wasn't there, I moved onto Timepiece which was just around the corner. A band was setting up but it was clear they wouldn't be playing for a while and there were very few people there at that point. So I resolved to come back later.

After that, I carried on my tour of the Roman City Wall, through Northernhay gardens, over the locked gate (yes I must have been manic) down the back of Harlequins, under the Iron Bridge and up the steps by the side of the Catacombs. Still in search of a good night out, I darted across Bartholomew Street and up Mary Arches Street to Mama Stones. The place was shut.

The only thing to do was to complete my tour of the wall, so I went back across the street, down through the Catacombs, up and down steps, up the path underneath Snell Tower, past the Picture House, down West Street and back onto the quay along the West side of the wall, above the Bishop Blaize.

When I got to the Prospect, I was in need of another drink so I went inside. Can't remember what I ordered, but the football was playing on the flat screen TV to the right. The table was empty so I sat down. A penalty was in progress and Balotelli was taking it. He looked directly into the camera and I thought he was seeking spiritual guidance from me. After a few seconds, he turned around, took the penalty and scored. I was so impressed I thought I would give him my jacket as a memento. So I took it off and left it on the chair on my way out of the pub. Thankfully the staff kept it safe and I was able to pick it up a few weeks later when I'd got my sanity back.

After that I picked up my Land Rover from the car park at work, with the intention of going back to Timepiece. The closest I could get was Queen Street, where I backed up against the gate to Northernhay Gardens that I'd climbed over earlier.

When I got to Timepiece again, it was packed. The band was playing and people were either watching or locked in private conversation. I picked my way to the bar where two women were blocking the way. I waited for them to move, but they didn't. I got the impression they were a pair of lesbians and it was clear which one was in charge. So I moved to another part of the bar and managed to get a coke.

After this, I watched the band and moved around to several places around the room, checking out the responses from everyone there.

When someone moved on, then I would too. I gave it half an hour or so, after which the band were done. I was disappointed that Madonna hadn't shown up, presumably preferring to stay in her hotel instead.

The next morning was a Saturday and I decided to go for a run. I took my phone and house keys with me, not knowing that I would soon be parted from them as a result of my ongoing manic behaviour.

Madonna was still in the back of my mind, but this did not seem relevant at this point, I ran all the way up Pinhoe Road, Blackboy Road and then down Sidwell Street and the High Street. When I got to the entrance of the Guildhall Shopping Centre, something made me stop. This was the trigger for me to bring on the delusional stuff and I decided to turn right.

Various people seemed to be reacting to me and I started following them, moving from one person to the next, to and fro. I walked as far as Sainsbury's turned right and then went past WH Smith, through the arcade and out onto Queen Street. That seemed to be the limit on how far I needed to go and I considered placing my phone on the ground at that point. I was imagining this as a kind of electromagnetic force transfer between the phone and the ground. In the event I decided against it and went back into the shopping centre.

Back at Sainsbury's again, I saw a kind of desk over by the lift. For some reason, my brain equated this with a banking system and I needed to deposit my keys to open the door to my new life. So I placed my keys there and left them.

When I got back onto the High Street again, there were several vans parked there including a TNT van. I thought this was an explosive device that needed a trigger, so I walked all the way round and then placed my phone on the pavement in from of the leading van. I then walked away onto Cathedral Yard.

At this point I was starting to get quite excited. I knew that the Royal Clarence is the oldest hotel in England and if Madonna was staying in Exeter it would be a sure bet she was there. So I walked into the hotel and asked about it in reception. I was given a piece of paper explaining all about the hotel and I asked if I could take a look upstairs. She said yes.

As I didn't have a room number, I was operating on pure intuition at this point. I checked out several room doors but didn't get any clues. Then finally I found a door that seemed to be "right". I was too scared to knock so I took the "do not disturb" sign off the handle. Then I heard a softly spoken female voice in my head which said that she was feeling sheepish and didn't want to take it any further at this point. I was both delighted that she was speaking to me and disappointed that she didn't want to meet face to face given we were only on opposites sides of a door.

I walked back along the corridor and was about to go down a set of stairs when a man appeared. He'd obviously been told I wanted a tour of the hotel and offered to take me downstairs through the kitchen to see the original parts of the building. From there a passage took me back out onto the street without going through reception. This made me feel like I was being shown the back door.

At that point I felt awful. I walked past St Martin's church and out onto what used to be Bedford Street. There I saw a police car, turned round and saw a van which said "Managing cash in society". I thought this was a comment about the way I was carrying on having a serious downside in terms of money. So I found a cafe and asked for a glass of water as I had no money on me.

I thought Madonna came into the cafe, but she didn't sit with me and either way I wasn't in the mood any more. I got more and more depressed in the cafe.

Then I went outside and wandered into Barclays Bank to see if any money would be forthcoming. I went back outside and by this time, the shopping centre security guards had been called because I looked suspicious. I was practically collapsing at this point. They said they would get help and I went with them inside an office somewhere. I curled up on the sofa and wanted to die.

The medical staff, when they arrived, didn't know what to make of me. I explained that I'd been for a run, got disoriented and lost my keys and my phone. Physical and mental exhaustion was the best they could come up with and it was agreed I would be taken to A&E by ambulance.

...

At A&E, I was sat on a chair, given some food and drink and I started to feel a bit better. So I agreed with them that I would go to the police station in search of my phone and keys.

In the event, I didn't want to leave the hospital. Having already collapsed once whilst out and about, I doubted that I would make it to the police station on another wild goose chase. So I wandered about inside, trying out beds that were parked in the corridors and stuff like that. I was getting hungry by that point so I went in the direction of the cafe, but I encountered two security guards before I got there.

They explained that I would not be getting any food if I didn't have any money and I explained that I didn't fancy going to the police station to get my phone and keys. I can't remember exactly what happened, but the net effect was I ended up back in A&E for a more detailed assessment.

This time I was in a cubicle and I could hear Madonna's voice through the monitor. Various doctors came and went. Some did tests, other tried to talk to me. I was given a drug which seriously did not agree with me because I can remember my brain speeding up, like what happened when I overdosed on the hash cake in Amsterdam. This triggered some seriously bizarre episodes where I was interacting with the security guards in a kind of David Lynch style movie. When I managed to get out of the cubicle and wander around, I was escorted back again. I think my Mum and Pete turned up at one point but they concluded I was loopy.

After that, a doctor from The Cedars turned up and it was agreed I would be taken into mental hospital for another extended stay.

When I was in hospital, my hallucinations and delusions continued. Maybe there was a link with the anti-psychotic medication because I'd reduced Quetiapine from 300mg to 100mg shortly before being admitted. And once inside I refused to take it at all for a couple of weeks so was on Lithium alone.

I carried on hearing Madonna's voice but only in selected places. To start with, this was next to paintings of a woman in purple and pink. There was one in the male lounge, one at the end of the male wing and another one at the entrance to the male / female wing. It was configured as a male wing to start with, so that was OK. I could stand next to it without fear of being moved on by the nurses.

Life in mental hospital consisted of the following things:

- Sleep
- Lounging around in bed
- Reading, puzzle books, whatever
- Pacing around in my room
- Pacing up and down the corridor
- Eating at meal times
- Getting a drink at other times
- Walking in the secure garden
- Getting leave to go outside the building

Some people liked to hang around in communal areas, listening to music or doing stuff in the creative room. But that generally wasn't for me.

There were also some scheduled activities in the activities centre, shiatsu massage, tai chi, walking group and breakfast club. I would take part in those when I felt well enough to do so, which on this occasion was not very often.

The main things for me were pacing around in my room and up and down the corridor because that's where I got to interact with the voices in my head. Very rapidly, I started to get additional voices in my head. Mark from work started giving me orders. As did his "boss" who was a fictional character invented by my brain. Mark had left to form a new company with Madonna and this man. They were filming my activities in a kind of Reality TV show.

I believed that they could both see and hear what I could see and hear. I thought the government must have implanted a device into my head when I was in hospital, most likely when I was unconscious for 3 days after taking an overdose. Which raised all sorts of questions in my mind as to the relationship between the government and this new private company. Sure enough, the voice of a military man appeared into the mix.

I could hear Mark, Madonna and the boss man inside my head from above, whereas the military man was from below. It could have corresponded with him being in the floor below, as this was a 2-storey building. Also it was not clear to me whether his voice was inside my head or outside. Either way, it was all very convincing. Right down to the foul language he used.

I would walk up and down the corridor, glancing to the left or the right under directions from Mark. The line of lights on the ceiling were targets for me to "shoot" at by blinking my eyes. Colours had a significance. Red meant escalating tensions all round. Blue meant average and green meant calming down. These corresponded to the colours of cups in the kitchen. I would pick one up and then go walking around with it, glancing at or touching objects of the same colour to enhance the effect.

After a while, I could hear more voices. The government took over my room, so there were voices in there giving me instructions and taking debriefings. Mark and the boss man were confined to the corridor.

I also got the message that Madonna and her entourage had taken residence. I could hear them in animated fashion across the courtyard. In my mind, this meant that winning the game show was all about finding Madonna and this propelled me to ever greater levels of manic behaviour inside the hospital.

At one point, I was scouting the female wing to see which room she was in. I even sat in the female lounge and banged on room doors, but she was never there. Predictably, I got banished by the staff. They became super-sensitive if I even strayed close to the entrance of the female wing.

After a while, the "shoot" behaviour led to me thinking that my blink response was sending out a pulse of electromagnetic energy. This gradually turned into a powerful laser-like effect and I was advised to keep my head down to avoid hurting anyone. So I would walk around looking at the floor, daring to look up just enough to see what was ahead. If I happened to momentarily make an eye-to-eye connection with anyone, Mark would say "boom", implying that they'd been injured.

This extended to when I was outside the building too. It was relatively safe on the grass between The Cedars and Wonford House, but if I strayed out onto the street, both cars and pedestrians had to be avoided. In between, they would set me tasks, which might be following people or cars. For cars in particular, there was a code of symbols. A learner driver was a comment on my abilities, basically meaning I'd got something wrong. Highway maintenance meant the end of the road, or basically turn around and go the other way.

On one day, I had leave to go to my mother's house. Apparently I was behaving so out-of-the-box that they sent me right back. From my perspective, I was just interacting with the voices in my head.

And I'd cycled down to Sue's house at 6am and knocked on the door because I thought I'd heard her in my head. This was explicitly against the terms of the Non-Molestation Order and sure enough Sue reported it to the police. I was let off on grounds of being insane.

On another day I can remember doing all sorts of crazy things in the street, to deliver a TV show with my eyes. I was following cars back and forth and standing by the kerb "directing" cars by sweeping a line on the road with my laser vision. By the end I even got into a couple of cars, thinking they were government agents and this was what I was supposed to go. Deepest apologies to whoever you were. I can honestly say this was when I was the most unwell. I was picking litter when the police found me and sent me back to hospital.

After some time, my relationship with Madonna went sour. It didn't matter what I did, she was never there at the end of the trail. I even kicked down a secure fire door and turned the contents of the metal cabinet upside down in the stairwell, to no avail. The anger and frustration led to me throwing a table at a window and pulling a lamp socket and wires out of the ceiling.

This meant the reality TV show was in difficulty and the focus moved from the activities of a private company to those of the government.

The main agent was also a woman. She had a softly spoke voice too, just like Madonna, but with a different accent so it was clear who was who. Madonna was relegated to the toilet and I could no longer hear her voice by the pictures in the corridor or lounge.

I asked about the nature of technology they'd implanted in my head and soon wished I hadn't. They demonstrated that just as I had laser vision with my eyes, they had remote control laser pain induction anywhere they liked throughout my body.

Things took a distinctly different turn when another female agent joined the fray. She had a voice like Madonna's but more gravelly. At the controls of the device, she aimed the pain at my penis. When it grew in response, she made the comment, "There, that's a better size". The effect was unavoidable, resulting in me sorting myself out in my room, for the first time in some time too. The trouble was, I was convinced that the whole world was watching. I asked how many and got the answer "2". I assumed that was the 2 female agents.

I also became aware that the voices in my head were responding to my thoughts, not just my speech and my actions. So I imagined they had a "Thought Machine" in addition to the "Zappy Machine". This was seriously disconcerting, because if I even thought a bad thought they would jump right onto it. I felt an incredible amount of pressure.

The next time they used the Zappy Machine, I asked how many were watching. This time I got the answer "40". This was seriously off-putting. I went and spoke to Madonna about it and she was aware what was going on, just not in a position to do anything about it.

At this point I kind of went off the rails, disobeying the voices in my head. It resulted in the military taking control of the Zappy Machine and that was the end of my relationship with Madonna too.

Barrack Obama Wanted Me to Report In

Once the military were in control, there was no doubt I was working for the government. They had me doing exercises, including running down to the barracks on Barrack Road and following trails of twigs on the grass. How I didn't get moved on I will never know.

They were initially very cautious about my vision. And they even accused me of shooting a helicopter when it passed overhead and I dared to look at it. However, the pilot regained control and this was taken as meaning that although it caused a disturbance, it was not so dangerous. So I was now focussed on looking people in the eye and seeing what response I got, both as pedestrians and driving cars. Many would look away, but some would stay the course and I realised that it was all completely safe.

Over time, the military did their evaluation of my capabilities. And the net result was that they weren't particularly interested. They thought it was too unreliable to use as a weapons guidance system because I couldn't keep my thoughts and my vision 100% accurately focussed on what they wanted me to do.

By this time, I was doing regular debriefings in my room, both to the military and to other government agents. The focus switched from my laser vision to my previous physics projects. I did a full presentation of everything I had done.

At this point, things escalated and I was asked to do a presentation with questions and answers to US Congress. Although my relationship had been with the British Military, it was clear that the US government was pulling the strings overall. So I did my presentation.
Finally there was a distraction in terms of a new admission to the hospital called "Star". She was 18 years old. She was introduced by the nurses and one of the first things she did was to organise everyone in the communal area. My job was to sit down in front of the door. I was spell-bound.

This resulted in Star appearing as a voice in my head, primarily when I was back in my room. This was the first occurrence I had of a voice corresponding to a real person in close proximity. I would talk to Star and then meet her in the corridor. At one point I wandered into what was now the female wing and talked to her outside her room. This was before I got banished by the nurses once again.

I would also talk to Star's voice in the communal area as that seemed to have a strong connection. Then sure enough she appeared and we went into the creative room to do some drawing. I drew what I saw outside the window and a picture of her too. I don't think she really knew what to say because I was old enough to be her dad. Being unaware of boundaries like this is another sign of mental illness.

And then I was asked to do a presentation for Barrack Obama. At that point, my thoughts betrayed me because I thought about the colour of his skin and that of Star's too. Given this was all hooked up to the Thought Machine it meant I was a racist. So I spent the next few hours explaining myself, as more and more thoughts uncontrollably leapt into my head. I complained loudly about the Thought Machine and that they should really turn if off given how unfair it was. And also complained about the Zappy Machine and asked for that to be switched off too.

Then I thought about the colour brown. My first car, which was a Vauxhall Cavalier sprung to mind. Then also did Claire's comment about it being "poo brown". Barrack was horrified. I was so distraught I virtually passed out on my bed.

The next time I met Star the subject of racism came up naturally in conversation and I was able to deal with that in a reassuring way.

The final time I remember meeting Star was in the dining room at lunchtime. I'd been hearing her voice all along the corridor and it even continued while I was stood right in front of her. So it was clear for the first time that the voice in my head and the real person were entirely different. This was the dawn of the end of my psychosis.

I carried on hearing voices for a while and kept on interacting with them but thinking more closely about who they really were. I went in town, thinking I had to buy a phone from the Apple Shop. Along the way, I stood for a moment outside the Church of the Latter Day Saints on Wonford Road. Then I encountered a couple of taxis with "Apple" printed down the side. So I followed them thinking they were significant. And I directed traffic with my laser vision down Topsham road. In the event, I couldn't buy an Apple phone so I bought 2 pairs of trainers from the shop next door. I would never normally go there. I then searched for an Android phone but gave up when I couldn't get a Google Nexus which was what I really wanted. Then I saw the Managing Cash In Society van as before and deemed the exercise was over.

When I got back to the hospital grounds, I was really frustrated. I didn't know whether the purchases belonged to me, or to the voices in my head who were clearly associated with corporate USA. So I threw them over the fence into the new building site. I also discarded my wallet as I had no idea who was bank-rolling my activities.

Inside, one of the nurses had seen what I'd done and collected my trainers. He said that these were my belongings and I should look after them. This was like music to my ears because it gave me a clear signal for what was real and what was not.

The next day, my thoughts had organised themselves to realise that I wanted my wallet back too. So I asked to go outside and retrieve it, which I did successfully.

All in all, I was fed up with the mess my hallucinations and delusions were causing. I was worn out. Even though I was still hearing multiple voices, I'd decided they were all fiction and I no longer wanted to hear them. So I made the decision not to listen to them and went to see the doctor, asking to be put back on anti-psychotic medication.

To my horror, they'd decided that they would use another drug called Depixol, administered by injection because they didn't trust me taking it orally. I objected but there was no way they were going to put me back on Quetiapine. So I agreed to go on Depixol and initially I was fine.

I have no idea what caused the voices in my head to disappear, but over the next few days they got quieter until finally they were gone.

When I returned to the community, I encountered Mark at work. I did a reality check to see if there were voices in my head and there were none.

Divorce in the Courts

Even once I'd dealt with the criminal conviction and got myself out of hospital, I still had the stress of a divorce process to deal with. It was costing me a great deal in legal fees, though thankfully I was saving an equivalent amount by staying with my mum.

Because of the Non-Molestation Order, there was no communication allowed between us and the usual mediation-type process was out of the question. So Sue hired a lawyer who specialised in injunctions and she started the divorce process that way instead. We would both fill in a monstrous Form E, then these would be presented to a judge and a judgement would be made. I was looking at an all-up bill of around £10k, which was ludicrous given how much I would likely be walking away with. However, I didn't have any choice, all because of police policy.

After multiple visits to my lawyer, we turned up in court and that was the first time I'd clapped eyes on Sue since the salsa incident. To cut a long story short, a judgement was reached and we were divorced soon afterwards. The thing was, I still loved Sue and didn't want to be divorcing her at all. I'd even asked the question via solicitor's letter whether she really wanted to go ahead with it and the answer was an emphatic yes.

I was genuinely surprised when we ended up talking again before the first payment to me had been made in accordance with the court order. That was a really nice thing to happen, but it coincided with exceedingly high stress levels because of the Depixol.

I ended up back in hospital, where they took me off anti-psychotic medication altogether. I thought that was a brave move, but it proved to turn out OK. It was under those circumstances that Sue met me for the first time since the violent incident. She deemed it to be a safe place, in a hospital with everyone else around and we managed half an hour together. Even this much was breaking the terms of the Non-Molestation Order, but I trusted her not to go and get me arrested. She even lent me a CD player with some soothing meditation-type music.

When I came out of hospital, I was off work for another week given how suicidal I'd become prior to admission. During that time, I voluntarily put myself back on Quetiapine because of the beneficial effects it has on my general stress levels and ability to sleep. Over time, I have reduced the levels to 100mg once more, only this time without any psychotic effects. I'm assuming the difference is that my general levels of stress have reduced, so there is nothing driving the psychotic process.

On my most recent visit to the consultant, he's taken the view that my mood level needs lifting a bit and so prescribed Lamotrigine, in addition to Quetiapine. I haven't taken any yet, but I am hoping the experience will be a positive one. I remain optimistic that the delusions and hallucinations have been left in the past.

Reflections

My relationship with Sue has been to hell and back, including divorce. In spite of everything I got back together with her again and thought things were looking up. Then she took the decision that she didn't love me and didn't want to be in a relationship with me anymore. I was absolutely heartbroken because I regard Sue as the love of my life.

Do I regret going to war? Yes I do. Because of the impact it had on Sue and also my eldest daughter.

Of course this is all with the benefit of hindsight and I know a number of things that I would not have found out otherwise. Also it did turn things around somewhat and put my on the front foot for a change. The trouble is that my behaviour has basically resulted in me being on my own.

Although I have an official diagnosis of Bipolar Disorder, I seriously wonder whether Borderline Personality Disorder would be a more accurate description.

In an effort to repair the relationship with my eldest daughter, after two and a half years of ignoring me, I have recently sent her a hand-written letter. This was as advised by my counsellor, Brian:

Dear Sweetheart,

I would just like to say that I still miss you. I know we had a big argument 2 years ago, which resulted in you staying round at your mother's house full time. For my part, I very much regret what happened and would like to say sorry.

As you know, I have been diagnosed with Bipolar Disorder which is a form of mental illness. I can see now that I was becoming progressively more ill leading up to the time that we had our argument. If I behaved in an aggressive way, shouting and waving my arms, made you scared or behaved in an excessive manner, then all of these are symptoms of the illness. This does not excuse what happened, but does help to explain it. Please accept my apologies for that. I am much better now.

In particular, I regret sending you home on your birthday and sending you back to Nanny Judy's when we were camping a year or so prior to that. I also regret the argument I had with your mother that led to her claim via the CSA and a DNA test for you. All of that could have been avoided.

I hear that you've done extremely well with school this year and hope that you get the exam results you deserve. I also understand that you're doing well with your first job at the Westbank, which is great to hear.

I miss the times we used to spend together, even if it was just driving you to see a friend in Mandy the Landy. I hope that somewhere deep inside you miss me too.

It would be lovely if we could spend some quality time together once again. I don't know what to suggest ... perhaps buying you a hot chocolate in a cafe and spending some time talking would be a good start?

Lots of love,

Dad

I am hoping for a response ...

Milton Keynes UK
Ingram Content Group UK Ltd.
UKHW010625040624
443705UK00001B/9